Patchwork

D0598579

AVERIL COLBY is the foremost authority on the technique, design and history of Patchwork. Here she has produced the definitive work on the subject. The book will appeal to a wide circle of needlewomen on account of its enchanting photographs and on account too of the fresh historical information which it gives about this traditional household craft. The book's chief aim, however, is the essentially practical one of helping workers to design and make their own Patchwork. To Miss Colby the craft is a living one and it is a part of her purpose to encourage its growth along the best lines of contemporary taste. She has therefore supplied full and easily understood working instructions on the practical aspects of Patchwork: on materials, tools and equipment, templates, colour and design, lining and finishing and applied work; and about the patches themselves, whether diamond, hexagonal, shell or of other shapes. These written instructions are expanded and clarified by more than 200 photographs, drawings and diagrams. Patchwork, like embroidery, is beginning to share in the revival of creative needlework in general. This book, as beautiful in its illustrations as it is helpful in its instructions, will give an additional stimulus to that revival.

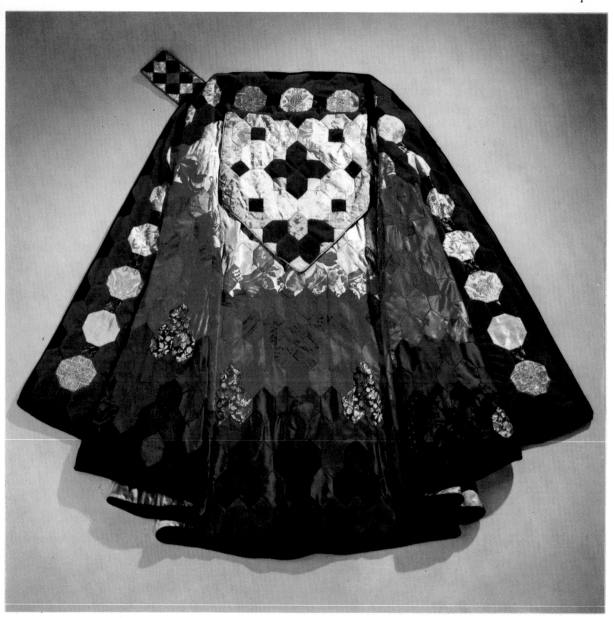

1 The cope made by parishioners of Burford, Oxfordshire (1954) to commemorate the Coronation of Queen Elizabeth II and given to the Parish Church. It is made of satin, velvet and brocade in black and shades of red, with green, gold, ivory and white. (p. 153)

AVERIL COLBY

Patchwork

B. T. BATSFORD, LONDON

© Averil Colby 1958
First published 1958
Ninth impression 1976: first paperback edition
Tenth impression 1978

Printed in Great Britain by litho by
The Anchor Press Ltd, Tiptree, Essex
for the Publishers B. T. Batsford Ltd,
4 Fitzhardinge Street, London W1H OAH
ISBN 0 7134 0392 6

*The front cover design is reproduced from a
cotton quilt (1810) containing a centre panel
printed from a polychrome woodblock,
designed to commemorate the Golden Jubilee
of George III, in colours of dark red and russet,
bright and dark blues, greens and canary yellow.
It is lined with calico and interlined with sheep's wool.*

PREFACE

Patchwork has been made in England now for two hundred and fifty years and, if I may borrow a phrase, is still going strong. It has naturally had its ups and downs in popularity and quality of design but not at any time does there seem to have been an artificial revival after a "down" period; perhaps it should be described as a "rest" period, as any re-starting has been spontaneous with no loss of vitality. In comparison with other kinds of needlework, very little has been written about patchwork and references to it in books, letters and family records are few and far between. Finding examples of the work itself has not always been a straightforward business, even when I have followed up local advice and hearsay as to its whereabouts. Quilts or coverlets appear sometimes in the most unusual places: in the potato shed covering the sacks in frosty weather is not uncommon; used as a dust-sheet on the mangle in the wash-house; spread over the family bicycles in the back-kitchen passage; or put *under* the mattress on the bed as a protection from rust on the springs beneath, are some of the misuses of patchwork. Worse still, is to track down a quilt only to be told that it had been "given to the rag-and-bone man" or just "cut up for rubbers". I have seen them used several times as a substitute for upholstery material on chairs—not as loose covers but stretched and nailed on with a professional touch. On the other side of the picture, there are the family treasures treated as heirlooms (and rightly so) —the everyday quilts and coverlets, one for winter, the other for summer, and the best quilts kept for visitors or other special occasions.

I have had the privilege of seeing wonderful collections of patchwork quilts in houses in the North of England and in South Wales, where they are considered indispensable, and for the opportunity to do so my thanks are due, not only to the generosity of their owners but also to Mrs Jack Fletcher of County Durham, Miss Anne Beveridge of the Northumberland Federation of Women's Institutes, Miss Thornborrow of Oxenholme, Westmorland, and Miss Mona Latham of Cumberland who helped me to find so much of the North Country work. Mrs Ramsden of Pembrokeshire did the same kindness for me in South Wales and both Mrs Elizabeth Hake and Mrs Mavis FitzRandolph generously allowed me the use of the notes they had made on the patchwork they saw while they were engaged on their researches into the tradition of English Quilting. I have felt overwhelmed by the generosity and confidence (not unmixed with responsibility on my part) which prompted so many people from all parts of the country to send their patchwork through the post for me to examine it at my leisure and have photographs taken.

Every illustration has been chosen to show more than one characteristic, each of which is typical of a period, a locality or a fashion and so on, so that full use could be made of them all. I only regret that so many others equally as good could not be shown for lack of space. Much of the interest in early patchwork depends on the period in which it was made, and for this reason I have included pieces which actually bear a date or for which there is good evidence of the approximate time at which it was made. It is a difficult matter to arrive at an absolute date for patchwork which has no record, but a knowledge of textile manufacture is a help, especially that of cotton printing. This is a specialised subject and although there are now many books dealing with textile printing, there is nothing like the actual comparison of fabrics in patchwork with others of a proven date. I have been fortunate, in connection with this side of patchwork, in having the help of Mr Peter Floud and Mrs Barbara Morris of the Department of Circulation at the Victoria and Albert Museum and of Miss Doreen Phillips of the Department of Textiles, all of whom have given me their advice on many of the quilts and coverlets I have collected. For this I am most grateful to them. Other museum authorities have been most generous with their help, especially Mr Ffransis Payne at St Fagan's Folk Museum, Cardiff, and Miss Jessie MacNab at the Castle Museum, Norwich, who have done research and looked out work for me, as also have the curators at Overbecks in Devon and Cotehele in Cornwall. Miss Anne Buck at the Gallery of English Costume in Platt Hall, Manchester, kindly produced advice and patchwork, both of which were very helpful, as also was the information on Canadian patchwork sent to me by Mrs K. B. Brett of the Royal Ontario Museum, Toronto.

There are still some gaps to be filled in the records of patchwork history in England, particularly during the first eighty years of the eighteenth century. With the exception of two pieces of work dated respectively 1708 and 1750 and a reference to patchwork in *Gulliver's Travels* in 1726, I cannot find anything which is authentic until about 1780. I have not been successful in tracing any of the patchwork which is known to have been made by, and was sold for, the Newgate prisoners. I have made enquiries in New South Wales which brought many delightful letters from people in Australia but no quilts. Mr F. R. Morrison, Acting Director of the Museum of Applied Arts, and Miss Phyllis Mander Jones, Librarian to the Mitchell Library, both in Sydney, most kindly undertook to do research and to make enquiries for me, but although it is certain that work was sold in New South Wales, none of it appears to have survived. Nearer to home and in spite of many enquiries, I have not discovered the whereabouts of the "Isle of Wight" coverlet (*131*) and only one piece of Shell patchwork (*113*), other than contemporary work, has appeared. I am convinced that there are yet many more examples of patchwork in different patterns from those already known waiting to be discovered in this country, but unless the search is continued until every box-room, linen-store, work-room, and attic is gone through and all old letters, family papers, diaries and wills are perused again, the whole history will never be complete.

Possibly this book may be the means of finding unknown work to add to that of which we already know and perhaps the patterns, and in many cases the humour, of the best work we possess may stimulate the present generation to do likewise for the future ones. I hope so.

The detailed diagrams and drawings will, I hope, make the various processes clear and I am immensely grateful to Norah Lee and Constance Truscott and thank them for their endless patience and the trouble they have taken to do them for me. Also to Mr Charles Burch for his help with the appendix dealing with making templates.

I should like to thank Miss G. M. Morgan for invaluable criticism and my especial thanks go to Mr Samuel Carr for all his kind advice and help in writing and preparing the manuscript and to Miss Muriel Rose without whose interest and help I should not have had the courage to tackle this book at all.

Langford,   Averil Colby
Somerset.
Spring, 1958

ACKNOWLEDGMENT

The author and publishers would like to thank the following for permission to reproduce the photographs included in this book:

John Arundell Esq., for fig. 155; Jane Austen Trust, for fig. 122; The Revd C. W. Harries, for fig. 141; Department of Archaeology, Government of India, for fig. 109; Manchester City Art Galleries, for fig. 123; National Museum of Wales, Welsh Folk Museum, for figs. 143, 156 and 163; Needlework Development Scheme, for figs. 182 and 183; Castle Museum, Norwich, for fig. 121; Mrs Fanny Rice, for fig. 128; Miss Muriel Rose, for fig. 131; Royal College of Surgeons of England, for fig. 152; Rural Industries Bureau, for fig. 142; The Trustees of the Victoria and Albert Museum, for figs. 112, 113, 115, 140 and 151; Weldon's Ltd, for fig. 149. The chair in fig. 105 was photographed by permission of the City Museum and Art Gallery, Bristol. The drawings in figs. 169, 170, 171, 172 were taken from photographs by permission of the Honble Rachel Kaye-Shuttleworth, Gawthorpe Hall, Burnley.

The author and publishers would also like to thank the following for kindly giving permission for their examples of patchwork to be photographed and included in this book:

Miss Avery, Orcheston St Mary, for fig. 161; Mrs Robin Bagot, Kendal, for fig. 110; Mrs Buchanan, Salisbury, for fig. 114; Mrs Cockburn, Currey Rivel, for fig. 154; Mrs A. M. Croft, New Milton, for fig. 157; Mrs Cruddas, Rookhope, for fig. 164; Miss Phyllis Dart, Teignmouth, for fig. 167; Mrs Deacon, Oxenholme, for fig. 176; Mrs Durie, Pensford, for fig. 158; The Misses Eggleston, Westgate-on-Weardale, for figs. 173 and 174; Mrs Elliott, Biggar, for fig. 111; Mrs Emerson, Bishop Auckland, for fig. 179; Mrs Erith, Dedham, for figs. 104 and 150; Mrs Campbell Gray, Cark-in-Cartmell, for fig. 166; T. L. Gwatkin Esq., Reading, for fig. 130; Mrs E. F. Hall, London, for the front jacket illustration; Miss Hall, Louth, for fig. 147; Mrs Henderson, Allendale Town, for fig. 178; Miss Josephine Howell, New York, for figs. 119 and 120; Mrs Japes, Mary Tavy, for fig. 129; Mrs Nathaniel Lloyd, Northiam, for fig. 180; Mrs Lowes, South Hanging Wells, for fig. 127; Miss Nixon, Stockfield-on-Tyne, for fig. 159; Mrs Osgood, Brentwood, for fig. 144; Mrs Joseph Emerson Peart, for fig. 177; Mrs Pentland, Ireshopeburn, for fig. 165; Miss Muriel Rose, Chelsea, for figs. 105 and 106; Miss Margaret Rowe, Bearsted, for fig. 145; The Revd Fairfax Scott-Tucker, Vicar of Burford, for the frontispiece; The Director of the Shakespeare Memorial Theatre for fig. 168; Mrs Stobart, Tow Law, for fig. 160; Miss Irene Synge, Ings, for fig. 139; The Misses Thornton, Derby, for fig. 124; Mrs Truscott, Watlington, for fig. 146; Walter White Esq., Bepton, for fig. 175; Mrs Wilson, Buckland Dinham, for fig. 125; Mrs Young, Elsdon, for fig. 162; Mrs Christine Bulmer, Hereford, for fig. 184.

CONTENTS

CONTENTS

LIST OF ILLUSTRATIONS

The Numerals in Parentheses in the text refer to the 'Figure numbers' of the illustrations

CHAPTER ONE

THE EARLY HISTORY

Thrift and careful living are part and parcel of rural life and it is in the cottages, farms and country houses that the greater part of English patchwork is to be found and where research is most rewarding. The country way of life sets the scene for work in which little account need be taken of time. For some it has provided the opportunity for creative work and achievement; for others the inevitable isolation has resulted in boredom and a longing for distraction and escape, but, whatever the reason, needlework has always played a large part in the lives of countrywomen.

In the thirteenth century English embroidery was known all over Europe and traditional quilting in England has an unbroken history of which we do not know the beginning. It is out of these two well-known kinds of needlework that the mosaic and applied patchwork grew with which we are now so familiar and which has added another charming chapter to English domestic crafts. The early history of patchwork is lost in time. There can be no doubt that it is as ancient as other kinds of needlework which, because of their simplicity and economy, were obviously of peasant origin.

The term patchwork has been associated, in a general way, with needlework in which fragments of cloth are used—either as pieces in a mosaic which are joined edge to edge by stitching or else applied as a decoration to the surface of a background material. The mosaic type is patchwork in its truest form, as it is used to construct the whole fabric. Written records are few and far between but patchwork is a more ancient occupation than can be proved by any record; it must have come before writing. The primitive necessity for repair would suggest the application of any available material to strengthen a worn place or to cover a hole; and if the worn fabric was part of a garment, pride in appearance would lead to the simple idea of making the patch appear as something decorative. As a means of repair it is not necessarily an unskilled operation, particularly on valuable fabrics.

Economy, for one reason or another, has always provided the stimulus for patchwork. In the early appliqué, pieces of rich and rare woven fabrics were used because they were too precious to throw away; embroidery silks were costly to buy and fragments of valuable cloth were employed as a substitute for embroidery, so making a double economy. Valuable materials were also saved for mosaic patchwork but the making of bed-furnishings from partly-worn clothing has flourished whenever materials have been cheap; if old garments could be replaced by new ones before they were too worn, and the pieces saved from them used to make a good quilt or coverlet, the whole transaction could be justified.

It is reasonable to assume that applied work was the earliest kind of patchwork because of its use in repair as well as decoration, although this cannot be proved. Probably the most ancient piece of applied work is that in the Boulak Museum in Cairo, dated about 980 B.C. It is a ceremonial canopy made of dyed gazelle hide cut in many of the different patterns used in the cartouches and symbols of Egypt. Some of them are still used in Egyptian applied work, although the material of the present day is cotton and the brightly-coloured designs include a characteristic use of black.

Decorative applied work, used as an economical substitute for embroidery, has flourished in many European and Asian countries. Often it was combined with embroidery stitches, which were used as a means of covering raw edges, as well as attaching the applied patterns to the background. Its value here is obvious, where strong colour and a pattern with a clear outline were needed.

Many excellent examples of ecclesiastical work, as well as house furnishings in appliqué, can be seen in private houses and museums in England and in other countries. Several historic pieces of early English applied work are shown in the country houses which are open to the public and perhaps the most exciting among them are the sixteenth-century panelled wall-hangings in Hardwick Hall in Derbyshire. A note on the materials used, taken from Mr Kendrick's *Book of Old Embroidery*, says that "there is a suspicion that some of the stuffs may have belonged to vestments no longer required for the service of the Church", but it does not say whether the Church was aware of this. The work was done by the Countess of Shrewsbury, "Bess of Hardwick", famous in her time for many things and not the least for her accomplishments as a needlewoman. Other examples of work in which the purpose was to preserve valuable fabric include some appliqué curtains in the private library of Corsham Court in Wiltshire. The applied pieces of embroidered crimson and cream satin and velvet were originally mule trappings and coverings for the state coach made by the ladies of Lisbon for Mr John Methuen while he was in Portugal from 1692 until 1705. The work was probably done soon after Nash had completed the new building at Corsham in 1805.

Applied work, as well as embroidery, was used in making banners and other heraldic devices in the Middle Ages and it is a method which has continued to the present day; some of the banners now made in the heraldic pattern differ very little from those carried in the Crusades. An interesting collection of simple heraldic banners was made in 1954, representing each of the counties in the Principality of Wales, and intended for display at the National Eisteddfodau and other occasions.

A method of doing applied work, in which the patterns have the freehand character of surface appliqué but are actually inlaid and so nearer to the mosaic patchwork, is seen in some Italian and Persian work. It is not strictly within the tradition of patchwork but nevertheless a cloth bed-cover made somewhat in this method is in the Folk Museum at St Fagan's Castle near Cardiff and an elaborate hanging is shown at Overbecks, near Salcombe in Devon.

It is a far cry from most of the early applied work to that which has become part of the patchwork tradition of the last two centuries but there is certainly a relationship which can be seen, in spite of the changes caused by fashion and circumstance. On the other hand, true patchwork has altered far less in construction and appearance from that which was done during the sixth and ninth centuries. Examples of this early work were discovered by Sir Aurel Stein's expedition earlier in this century, while making an archaeological survey for the Indian Government in the remote regions of Serindia, which lie beyond the Ganges.[1] A walled-up chapel was found in the Caves of the Thousand Buddhas, situated on the old trade route which ran from the silk-growing provinces of China into Central Asia and the West. There was a large collection of textiles in the chapel and among them several pieces of mosaic patchwork, which are remarkable in their likeness to some of the work done in the last hundred years. One large piece—described as a votive hanging—is made up of rectangular pieces of many-coloured and figured silks, damasks and embroideries (109). The pieces were probably votive offerings left at the shrine by travellers, many of them only rough fragments of silk which, in the case of the poorest people, were torn from their clothing. Other work found in the caves includes patchwork tops for banners and a small silk bag, possibly used to carry relics. The bag is made of patches in squares and triangles, which in shape and pattern are very like a Victorian bag made about 1890. In a description of this work[2] it is suggested that the maker was a man, presumably one of the priests at the shrine, who must also have made the hanging. The pattern is very simple, being in three rows of patches; the top and bottom rows of triangles in red and blue and the middle row in squares of ivory and triangles of green silk. The importance of the hanging and the bag is in their relationship to the work of any period made in England. The method of joining the patches by over-sewing the edges on the wrong side is identical with the technique used to-day and the shapes of the patches and the

[1] *Serindia*, Sir Marc Aurel Stein, O.U.P., 1921.
[2] *Needlework through the Ages*, Symonds and Preece.

patterns made by them are as familiar now as they were then. This example of pattern and stitchery was not discovered until the twentieth century and it does seem possible that other work may have survived in some other place, yet to be found, which will add a little more to a very sketchy story.

In her book Miss Symonds also mentions the possibility of patchwork having been known at the time of Rameses III and gives as evidence a wall-painting at Thebes of an Egyptian sailing boat. The sails appear to be made of squares of coloured fabric joined in a check pattern, with other pieces arranged in strips forming a chevron pattern round the border.

The first and only reference to an early patchwork bed cover occurs in a book of French poems or lays of the twelfth or thirteenth century.[1] The poem "La Lai del Desiré" tells the story of the immortal seeking the love of a mortal maid and being helped by the fairies and magic to win her. All goes well and the lady is led to a leafy bower where, preparatory to the nuptials—"The bed was prepared of which the quilt was of a check-board pattern of two sorts of silk cloth, well-made and rich". This nearly-literal translation from the period in which the lay was written leaves no doubt of the patchwork nature of the quilt. It may well be that the border was made of appliqué—the last line reads (in literal translation) "Around appears the new flower". No further mention is made in the lay and after this solitary contribution to the early domestic tradition of patchwork, there is another gap in recorded reference for several hundred years.

It is disappointing to find little early history of a social development of which there has been such a strong revival for more than two hundred years. Early references, because they are so few and so widely scattered, appear to be slightly out of focus and unreal. Looking back at the discoveries of each orphaned object, one has a feeling that something more must appear, but so far the long periods of separation remain until we come to the eighteenth and nineteenth centuries. When the scene shifts to England and the United States of America, it is much nearer to being "within living memory".

Many books have been written in America on the patchwork made in that country; so many in fact that it is not necessary to do more than to note certain of the facts which have been given. In the introduction to the booklet issued by the Newark Museum in New Jersey,[2] Margaret E. White says about Quilts: "Their story begins with the first settlers of New England and New Amsterdam, for the introduction of patchwork into America is credited to the thrifty English and Dutch colonists." It is frequently taken for granted, when writing of the seventeenth-century quilting in America, that the quilts were made of patchwork

---

[1] *Les Lais del Desiré, Groelent et Melion*, edited by Margaret E. Grimes.
[2] *Quilts and Counterpanes in the Newark Museum.*

but there is no evidence to support this. It is certain that the art of quilting was taken from England with the first colonists at that time but no mention is made of patchwork in any recorded work. In her study of traditional quilting Mrs FitzRandolph says ". . . the making of mosaic patchwork . . . became so popular with the American colonists and their elaborate designs are so famous, that American writers are apt to assume that the mention of a 'quilt' implies pieced or applied work".[1]

The association of the two words "patchwork" and "quilt" has become so familiar within the last hundred years or so that they have been generally accepted as inseparable. This is not so by any means. Much patchwork is unquilted and "plain quilts" of uncut material have a tradition of their own, which is longer than that of patchwork in England or America. References to quilts are found in lists of household goods as early as 1692, but Mrs Finley[2] gives the years between 1775 and 1800 as those during which the earliest surviving quilts were made. Mrs Hall, another American writer on the subject, illustrates in her book a quilt in the "Feather Star" pattern which was made in 1771.[3] The Americans set great store by their tradition of patchwork and justifiably so; certainly more attention and importance is given to patchwork quilts and coverlets there nowadays than in any other country, except perhaps Canada.

A characteristic of the American background to the work in its early days was the "Quilting Bee"—a party which was given when the patchwork was done and friends and neighbours were invited to take part in the final work—when the quilt was put into a frame and the quilting patterns stitched. A dower chest was not considered complete without a baker's dozen of quilts; the first twelve were made from the time a girl could sew well enough; the thirteenth was the bridal or marriage quilt and at the party called for the quilting of it, the betrothal was announced.

A typical American way of making a quilt is that in which the work is made up in sections or "blocks" to simplify the sewing and so many of the American patterns are exactly identical with a number which are traditional in the Northern Counties of England that it is reasonable to think that the original patterns first went out from Durham, Cumberland, Northumberland and Westmorland. It is impossible to illustrate all of them but some which are alike on both sides of the Atlantic are shown (*157, 159, 164, 166, 174, 176, 177, 178*). Some of the earlier quilts at the beginning of the nineteenth century contain English textiles which are of the same designs as the chintzes used in patchwork made in this country

[1] *Traditional Quilting.*
[2] *Old Patchwork Quilts and the Women who made them.*
[3] *The Romance of the Patchwork Quilt in America.*

at the same time. The early block and applied work patterns have maintained an unbroken popularity in America but the economical "scrap" or crazy work and the all-over mosaic designs never seem to have held the same place in the affections of the workers.

The importance given to the names of patchwork patterns is another characteristic of American work; the same pattern may be given many different names, according to the locality in which it is made, and a number of others recall popular political figures or great national events. Mrs Finley devotes a chapter of her book to what she describes as the "Migration of Patterns" and another to the origin of quilt names. One pattern which took its name from the small bean of a plant known as "Job's Tears" became "The Slave Chain" twenty-two years later, and in another twenty years—during the annexation of Texas—it had become "Texas Tears". After the Civil War, when civilisation spread to the West, the same pattern became known as "The Rocky Road to Kansas" and "Kansas Troubles", and by 1880 it appeared as "The Endless Chain"—a not inappropriate name for a pattern which had survived for so many years. Another pattern has collected the following names: "Indian Trail", "Forest Path", "Winding Walk", "Rambling Road", "Climbing Rose", "Old Maid's Ramble", "Storm at Sea", "Flying Dutchman", "North Wind", "Weather Vane", "Tangled Tares", "Prickly Pear", and "Irish Puzzle".

No doubt many of the patchwork patterns (as well as the quilting ones) travelled back across the Atlantic to the country of their origin with the addition of local and topical variations in name and design, and also new patterns which had grown out of the old; a needlework pattern is often a family heirloom and many such must have made the journeys across the sea.

The origins of patchwork in Canada lie in the origins of its people—the British Isles and France and after the American War of Independence, the United States of America. There was a wave of settlers from America at the end of the eighteenth and the beginning of the nineteenth centuries, who left their homes in the states as they wished to remain under British rule and they took their crafts with them. Many of the designs of patchwork made in Canada are common to both England and America and have gone to Canada from either. Certainly nothing has gone to either of them *from* Canada. A type of patchwork which has grown up in Ontario is one made of scraps of hand-spun, home-dyed and hand-woven checked and striped woollens. They are very utilitarian and very simple in arrangements of blocks of cloth but are gay and decorative in colouring. Designs which are popular in Canadian patchwork and those which are most typical are very much the same as the ones which are common to English and American work.

There is no longer the original need for quilts to be hand-made but the tradition is still a living one on the other side of the Atlantic. Women's magazines and commercial firms concerned with the necessary materials issue colour charts, illustrations, patterns and working directions—even to the amount of material needed in each colour—for doing the work. It seems that in this development, there is a danger to the natural and spontaneous spirit which is so essentially part of patchwork. The competitions in local and State fairs held up and down the country in both Canada and America, as well as those sponsored on a national scale by the Press, may preserve the liveliness of the old work as long as there is discrimination in the adjudication; but it is evident, generally speaking, that neither the sewing nor the designs are as good as they were a hundred years ago. In spite of this, patchwork probably owes its existence to the fact that it has never had any real commercial value. From time to time fashionable textiles have been printed in imitation of patchwork patterns but the time taken to make a true patchwork quilt which would show a reasonable profit to the worker has kept this traditional work entirely safe from the money-making business. On the other hand, if it had ever entered the trade as other country crafts have done, there would at least have been all the transactions and business dealings kept for reference, on which to build up a more substantial record than is possible to-day.

CHAPTER TWO

MATERIALS

At one time or another, almost every kind of manufactured material has been used for patchwork and applied work. Occasionally leather is found and the canopy made from pieces of gazelle hide in the Boulak Museum in Cairo is famous; in more recent years leather pieces have been made into rough bags for household use and floor rugs of sheepskin cuttings are serviceable as they wear and wash well. The lasting quality of all patchwork depends on its materials. It is a generally mistaken idea that "anything will do for patchwork"; there is no more work involved than in any other comparable kind of needlework but its piecemeal nature needs good basic quality in the stuffs used. Any which do not lend themselves to folding and seaming are better put to some other use.

The earliest materials known to have been used for patchwork in England were the "painted callicoes" or "chints", first imported from India in the seventeenth century. The introduction of these gaily coloured cottons revolutionised the English textile trade in woollen and linen manufacture; their cheapness and colour took the public fancy and women, who had dressed previously in woollen cloth, were "now clothed in calico and printed linen". After many protests and disturbances from the English weavers, restrictions and embargoes were imposed on the import of the fashionable cottons, but the effect of this was to make them more popular than before; one way after another was found to evade the restrictions, and though prices rose considerably, "charming chintz" continued to be worn. It was popular also for furnishings but because of the prohibitive prices not everyone was able to indulge in this fashion. Those who could not found another way and from the inevitable pieces (too precious to throw away) which were left from cutting out the shaped sleeves and bodices, a new fashion grew for furnishings made of patchwork. Four-poster beds were universally used and in spite of the task of making two pairs of curtains, a coverlet and valances, we know that this work was carried out, from many examples which have survived.

It has been thought that patchwork was unrelated to upper-class fashion, but comparing the early work with that done from about 1810 onwards, it seems that this was not so. The introduction of patchwork to village life in the eighteenth century came, probably, through the village dressmaker who went to the "big house" to work, or through the village girl who was in service there. Judging by pieces of chintz and fine cottons among the more ordinary dress prints, a number of coverlet materials began in a different walk of life from that in which they ended. Many quilts and coverlets were made as heirlooms and never meant for regular use, and from these little worn examples we can learn a great deal of the early materials, especially in work which has been wrapped and cherished since it was made. "Best" quilts were usually kept in a sheet—one was in a bandana when it was found (*145*)—and North Country work is almost invariably kept in a pillow case.

In the days of large families, dressmaking pieces were plentiful and it has been a common custom for a mother to make a quilt for each of her daughters, and very often for her sons. The girls have not necessarily made their own quilts (as in America), although they helped with the work. The time needed to make a quilt depended on the circumstances of the household; in families where everyone took a hand (including the father and sons) two or three would be made during a winter, but it would mean steady work for a single-handed worker to do it in that time—although it would depend on the size of the pieces used, the simplicity or otherwise of the design, the leisure time or industry of the maker and the urgency of the need for a bed covering. In many homes it has been customary for a stock of plain and patchwork quilts to be kept ready for use.

Dating work of any kind adds much to its interest and this is especially true of patchwork, but all too rarely is it dated by the maker; initials, with or without a date, are sometimes embroidered or written on some part of the work, but, generally, the only guide to its age is the materials it contains. Even so, the date can only be approximate, as it is usual for the materials to be collected over a period before the work is begun and they are, therefore, older than the finished patchwork. When several years of fashion are represented in one quilt, the last year's materials may indicate the date of completion. Unfinished work is difficult to date, as it may have lain for many years after the original worker had died and been completed by a later owner with materials of another period. Quilts are sometimes left with pieces which were meant to be used, as happened with the unfinished coverlet of late eighteenth-century cottons, illustrated in Miss Gertrude Jekyll's book *Old English Country Life*.[1] Some years after it was written, a bundle of pieces chanced to fall into the hands of someone interested in patchwork; much to her delight she found this actual coverlet among them, still unfinished, and was able to complete it with its intended pieces.

Finished quilts with documented pedigrees are often cherished by succeeding generations of one family; these are useful for comparing with others which have become orphaned and with no birth certificate, but unless it is actually dated, only an approximate period can be put on any patchwork. Nearly all the eighteenth-century work which remains is made from cotton, linen or calico—sometimes all together in one coverlet—but only a few pieces of silk patchwork seem to have

[1] 1926 edition.

survived and some of these just by the skin of their teeth. One fragment is supposed to have been made about 1710, a very worn quilt in 1750 and a silk-embroidered silk and velvet quilt dated as "late eighteenth century" is in the Victoria and Albert Museum. Perhaps if silk had had the long-wearing quality of the cottons of that time we should have had more of it in patchwork but the practice of loading silk shortened its life considerably. Some pure silk materials are in relatively good condition, compared with the tattered remains of those manufactured when loading or weighting became more general, towards the end of the eighteenth and during the nineteenth centuries.[1]

There is evidence that homespun woollens were made into rough patchwork in Scotland from the middle of the eighteenth century (p. 101) and cloth or "stuff" quilts were made before the middle of the nineteenth century in wool-manufacturing districts of England; moth and constant use have removed all traces of any but the later work.

Patterns and processes in cotton printing make it possible to put more accurate dates on many old quilts whose age previously had been unknown or only guessed. Alternatively, old patchwork has sometimes been the means of identifying printed designs. It is not possible in this book to give more than a few of the characteristics of the materials used in old patchwork but so many quilts are made from printed cottons that a closer study of these materials, in museums and in books which have been written especially on the subject, will give a "new look" to some of the less appreciated patchwork in the country.

The Levens Hall quilt is apparently the only one left now made from the imported Indian calicoes. The colours and some of the patterns are described in Chapter IX and illustrated (110). They are typical not only of the traditional Indian native painted calicoes, but they can be recognised as the inspiration of the many floral and leaf designs printed in England during the next hundred years; the patterns for hangings, curtains and counterpanes were somewhat heavier than those for dress fabrics, which were smaller and more formal. The early cottons are coarser than those of later years and can be distinguished by a "rough" feeling to the touch; it is difficult in small patches to tell the difference between linen and calico.

Until 1752 English textile printing had been done by means of wood-blocks, but in this year engraved copper plates were first used in Ireland and the innovation quickly spread to England. Wood-blocks were not superseded by the new process and both methods continued to be used. Early designs done by both methods are easy to distinguish; the drawing on the copper-plate patterns is finer

[1] Loading is a manufacturing process in which a substance such as shellac is added to silk to give a false impression of weight and thickness.

and the detail more delicate than on wood-blocks, and the close engraving lines can be seen in the coloured patterns. Plate-printing was possible only in one colour at a time, and characteristic colours are deep-toned shades of red, blue, sepia and purple. Block designs were gayer than the sober monochromes and included all shades of red, pink, indigo, purple, rich and pale yellows and olives and brownish greens, drearily known as *drab* but in reality beautiful colours. Vegetable dyes were used and the rather "rusty" black is easy to distinguish from the later and chemical jet-black dyes. Colours were often added to the early patterns by hand, by a process known as "pencilling". It was done (often by girls) to save expense in printing but not with great accuracy and where it has been used the colour has over-run the outline of the drawing. This shows clearly in a blue-flowered patch of calico, in the detail of a rosette pattern (*106*). Yellow was also added over blue to produce green but it faded in time, leaving only the blue. Unless much study has been given to the subject of cotton printing it is not easy to distinguish between all the different processes sufficiently well to put a date on any materials. Sometimes it is possible to see where colours have been over-printed, especially green. A single process for printing "solid" green was invented in 1809 but with the exception of a small group of monochrome roller-prints produced after 1820, there is practically no evidence of this process being in common use until about 1835. Printing by mechanical rollers was introduced in 1783 but it was not generally used until 1815, although printing was much quicker by this method. It is, again, difficult to tell the difference between these and hand-block prints on a small patch, but roller prints show identical repetition of any irregularities or flaws in the pattern, whereas hand-block prints rarely contain repeated mistakes. Later prints have the patterns put on by both processes.

Sprays and trails of floral designs lent themselves to patchwork shapes, and those with dark backgrounds (fashionable during the last few years of the eighteenth century) give a period character to many coverlets made then and in the early years of the nineteenth century.[1] A coverlet made in Westmorland about 1795 has a good collection of dark prints (*114*). Every kind of bright colour was used on many prints which had a natural or white ground, as well as those with dark grounds; many at the beginning of the nineteenth century had terra-cotta, red and yellow grounds (canary yellow was the "last word" about 1810), and by 1807 the "drab" colours had almost disappeared from printing, although they are found in patchwork for about another ten years. By the early 1800s, flower and leaf patterns began to look very "English"; the stylised flowers of the Indian prints still showed their influence in the trailing patterns, but many furnishing

[1] *The Chintz Book*, MacIver Percival, Plate XXXII.

chintzes were closely patterned with lush growths of roses, lilies, convolvulus, peonies and passion-flowers. A passion-flower chintz of the very early nineteenth century is illustrated in a section of the Brereton bed hanging (*121*).

Dress prints were used a great deal; as well as floral designs, many small "spot" patterns are found in nearly every coverlet made about this time. The background colours are often dark with a small repeating leaf, flower or formal pattern in pink, blue, lilac, drabs and white. White or light-coloured grounds are printed with the same kinds of patterns in dark colours.

Enthusiasm for patchwork amounted to a craze by the beginning of the nineteenth century. Ladies with the time to spend sat all day doing patchwork; a Miss Hutton (born in 1756), who lived to be ninety, wrote an account of her needlework labours in which she said she had "made patchwork beyond calculation". By the 1850s the fever had not abated and we know that in cottage homes the children were set to work almost as soon as they returned from school: "As soon as the lamp was lighted, out came the patchwork." An old lady who lived to be eighty is said to have made a patchwork quilt for every year of her life by the time she died early in the 1900s. We are not told what she did with them all. Visitors and relations who came to stay were also turned on to do their daily contribution to the work in hand.

In 1800 cottons were cheap to buy; "printed cottons" were two shillings a yard and a few years later the "new-printed chintzes" could be bought for seven or eight shillings a yard according to quality. Everybody who was anybody had a coverlet (quilts were "out" as far as fashion went, although they never ceased to be made) and the really stylish affair had an elaborate and striking centre design. Cotton manufacturers printed decorative panels from 1800 until about 1816, designed especially as centre panels for the fashion-conscious makers of patchwork. They must have sold by the hundred, as those remaining to this day in quilts can be counted almost by the dozen. They were extremely colourful and some of them very pretty; the designs included garlands and bouquets or baskets of flowers or fruit (or both) enclosed in a formal shape and surrounded by a decorated border. The shape and size of the panels varied; many were oval or round and even more took their cue from the patchwork shapes and were hexagonal, octagonal or square. Furthermore the factories produced special chintz borders to match those round the panels which were put into the "framed" quilts or as a final border to the whole pattern. The quilt illustrated on the jacket shows one of the decorative panels. This one was printed to commemorate the golden jubilee of George III in 1810 and contains a basket overflowing with a profusion of lilies, roses, convolvulus and marigolds in their natural colours, set in a ground of dark mahogany red. A border of brown acorns and green oak leaves is set in a ground of the "new" canary yellow. Below the basket and on the border the inscription "G – 50 – R" is flanked by the Rose of England and the Thistle of Scotland and the space below the inscription is filled with an impressive bunch of Shamrock, no doubt in celebration of the recent Act of Union with Ireland.

After Nelson's victory in the Battle of the Nile in 1897, the streets of Naples were decked with flags and streamers to welcome his return; among them were banners of blue-printed white cotton, on which the name "NELSON" was surrounded by a design of acorns and oak leaves. Pieces of this cloth were brought home by a young naval officer and used in a patchwork coverlet begun in the same year and finished in 1805, after Trafalgar. A coverlet made about 1817 (now in North Wales) contains a centre square printed with the figure of Admiral Collingwood (Nelson's successor), but this was probably printed as a commemorative handkerchief. A colourful block-printed panel celebrated Wellington's victory at Vittoria in 1813 and a small panel was also printed at the time of the marriage of the much-loved Princess Charlotte in 1816 and used in quilts up and down the country, as many can still be found. The floral panel is surrounded with the inscription, PRINCESS CHARLOTTE OF WALES MARRIED TO LEOPOLD PRINCE OF SAXE COBURG MAY 2 1816.

Appliqué patterns of the 1800s included many of the "game-bird" prints which were produced between 1814 and 1816; the "Palm-tree and Pheasant"[1] and the bird "conversation piece"—the "Plum-tree and Partridges"—are shown in two illustrations (144, 131). A rural scene with swans is in the centre of an English coverlet, now in the United States of America (120). Designs of printed cottons were influenced by the revived Chinoiserie fashion from 1805 onwards and are found in borders of framed quilts (120) and cut-out appliqué patterns (129). Roses were especially loved in chintz designs and can be seen in every quilt with a floral pattern until the middle of the century. Muslin was used for the high-waisted gowns of the late Georgian period and a now-fragile coverlet made from them about 1830 in *brick* pattern is illustrated (146).

The 1774 Act required cotton manufactured in England to have three blue threads woven into the selvedge for identification by the Excise authorities; not all English-made cottons had this mark but on those which had it does make certain that the cotton was English and that it was manufactured before 1811, when this provision was abolished. Other dating can be established by Excise stamps and makers' or factory names stamped on the cottons; these marks sometimes can be found on the hems at the backs of coverlets.

Ghosts of the Regency prints continued to haunt patchwork until about

[1] *The Chintz Book*, MacIver Percival, p. 30.

1850, but some cottons printed after the early 1830s are also ghost-like, due to the fading of the chemical dyes, rather than because they are relics of a past age. Floral furnishing prints almost disappear from quilts and small-patterned dress prints, sateen, poplin and Turkey twill take their place. *Weldon's Practical Publications* (1885) recommended "blue linen of the kind used for butchers' coats" and Turkey twill that "keeps bright and fresh to the last"; "Paisley" prints were also prized for their bright colours and were used for linings as well as the patchwork. Chintzes in traditional floral designs continued to be printed throughout the century but few are found in quilts after 1850. Some of the "broken scroll" and "fern" patterns appear in quilts made in the 1860s; a print designed towards the end of the nineteenth century was used about 1920 to repair the border of a coverlet made in the early 1820s (*139*). A square of cotton bearing Queen Victoria's head (a commemorative print for Jubilee year) was used in a coverlet about 1899; another floral print (1850) contained the profiles of the Queen and Prince Albert outlined by tendrils in the pattern. It is said that the Queen added the tendrils herself, when the design was submitted for her approval.

Cloth of all kinds was used for patchwork from the middle of the century; quilts, couvre-pieds and table-covers ("left on when the white cloth was spread, to protect the table from the hot dishes"); borders for table-covers "mounted on an olive green centre" were said to be "handsome" and we are told that "slippers and footstools worked with cloth or velvet are very comfortable and useful". So now we know. Cloth patchwork is said frequently to be made from "soldiers' uniforms", presumably of mess-jacket facings and not regular service uniform. The work being done by Private Thomas Walker (*152*)—obviously in felted cloth—suggests that this use of Government property was not altogether frowned upon when good cause for it could be shown.

The fashion which decreed stiff materials for dresses (skirts which stood out, gathered or pleated flounces and leg-of-mutton sleeves) from the middle of the century meant that most silk and satins were loaded and not strong enough to be used with anything heavy, such as velvet. The result of combining these kinds of dressmaking pieces is only too apparent in the tattered wrecks of what were once "Victorian" quilts. Those made in good silks are still in good condition and among them are the double-sided quilt illustrated (*151*), one in pale-coloured silks at Cotehele, St Dominic in Cornwall and a family heirloom in Hampshire, in silk, satin, brocade and authentic pieces of velvet from the length woven for Queen Victoria's coronation robe.

Bags, cushion and footstool covers, and antimacassars were made in velvet only, from about 1860; most are in good condition but as velvet is virtually unwashable, some are far removed from godliness. Ribbons and strong braid were used in *log-cabin* quilts; China ribbons were used for embroidery in *crazy work* and the flower sprays and border pattern on Jenny Jones' coverlet were so embroidered (*163*).

The main source of supply for patchwork pieces has always been remnants left over from furnishing and dressmaking and much of the sentimental attachment to the work lies in the use of once-familiar materials, although there seems to be little foundation for the stories of quilts made from wedding gowns. Twelve patches of royal blue satin came from the wedding dress of Mr White's mother (*175*) and a scrap of velvet in Jenny Jones' quilt is labelled "Father's Wedding Vest" (*163*). Patchwork made by or for children is often made from their dresses; a coverlet illustrated (*184*) was made for a child of twelve from her cotton dresses and about 1900 in one preparatory school each girl had a quilt made mostly from her dresses. (The boys' clothes were not considered suitable for patchwork and scarlet blankets were provided for them as a manly alternative.)

As well as home-produced pieces and those from the village dressmaker, out-of-date furnishing, tailor's and dress patterns have been obtained from textile trade houses for over a hundred years. They are unused and so are better wearing and many ready-cut patterns can be used without further shaping as in the *brick* pattern (*146*) and *zig-zag* quilts (*173*). Factory or warehouse bundles, short lengths and remnants are still sold in the markets and "fent" shops of Midland and Northern manufacturing towns. "Fents" are left-over pieces from factory or bankrupt stock and are sold in any length from a few inches, often for less than half the cost price. Bundles of odd-shaped pieces are sold by weight from one to five shillings a pound. About forty years ago border-check patterns from woollen factories were made into blankets; shirting patterns were collected for quilts made entirely of them, and sad-looking things they were. The best value for money which can be remembered now is that of a woman who used to be sent to the village shop about seventy years ago to buy "a pennyworth of patches all done up in a bag ready to be stitched together".

A preliminary washing of all new materials, if they are to be sewn to used pieces, will test them for shrinkage and "fast" colours; those with a glazed finish will lose their gloss but many new cottons have a permanent shine which is not affected by washing. It is important that the weight and texture of materials in one piece of work should be as nearly similar as possible; it is a mistake and uneconomical to put together different kinds of material. Some heavy cottons, such as casement, wear well with linen of the same weight; other cottons with finer linens go well together, especially with calico, twill, marcella, piqué, sateen, damask and so on. Silk and satin need to be of superlative quality to wear well; velvet is troublesome to handle but when it is used with first-quality silk, satin and brocade the result can be fit for a king. Most rayons are too "springy" to fold neatly enough for the precision of geometrical shapes, and the cut edges fray; the wholly synthetic materials (so far) are too transparent and generally unsympathetic to patchwork techniques and processes. The best of the contemporary materials are the glazed or semi-glazed furnishing and dress cottons. From the evidence of all the old work, linen and cotton textiles lend themselves well to the shapes and patterns and have been the most hard-wearing of any other materials, and there seems to be no reason why present-day linen and cotton should not last as long, if the quality is good to begin with. New materials are generally reliable but trade patterns often are holed where the bundles were clipped together; used materials need testing for thin and worn places and a simple method for doing this is to hold the pieces against a window-pane and draw a pencil line around any weakness which can be seen—it can then be avoided easily when cutting out.

Whatever the means of collecting the pieces—whether given, bought, acquired or mysteriously come by—it is important not to begin working without having collected enough to complete the pattern. It is permissible to buy small pieces when needed to complete a piece of work but it is against the tradition to buy *all* the materials and calls to mind Maggie Tulliver's views on all patchwork in *The Mill on The Floss*—"It's foolish work," said Maggie, with a toss of her mane, "tearing things to pieces to sew 'em together again."

CHAPTER THREE

TOOLS AND EQUIPMENT

The usual contents of a workbox—needles, thread, pins, scissors and thimble—together with selected pieces of otherwise unwanted materials, and templates for shaping the patches—are all that is needed for patchwork.

TEMPLATES

In early patchwork the shapes were made without templates; materials were folded and cut by the thread; but with the introduction of more ambitious shapes than squares or rectangles (such as six- or eight-sided pieces), it is not unlikely that this led to the need for a basic pattern. Quilting patterns relied on templates for ensuring the accurate repetition of an outline, and the idea of using them for patchwork may well have come from the traditional quilters. It is very necessary that patchwork templates are made of a hard substance that is resistant to scissor cutting, if they are not to lose their shape. Nineteenth-century templates were cut from oak, tin and card; others have been made from zinc, pewter, silver, brass and copper and one or two of bone and ivory have been found in old workboxes. Metals such as zinc and aluminium should be treated with caution, as templates made of both are likely to shave off at the edges with use; stiff card is good for temporary use but it, too, will become inaccurate with hard use. (Hard usage includes lending.)

Many old templates were home-made by the men of the household; they were always well and accurately cut and for present-day cutting at home, instructions are given in Appendix A. It is now possible to buy commercially produced plastic templates, and also some in thin Perspex which can also be cut at home, but no substance is as good wearing as brass or copper. Until the late 1920s templates had been used only for the basic shapes from which the paper patterns had been cut; a second template, used as a guide for cutting materials with accuracy also, was introduced into work done by Much Hadham Women's Institute with the help of Miss Muriel Rose (2, 3, 4, 5). This meant that templates were used in pairs, with the one for cutting materials approximately a quarter of an inch larger on each side than the basic shape. It will be seen from the diagrams that the large templates are shaped like a frame; this has the convenience, when laid on material, of showing the effect of the finished patch before cutting is done (*193, 196*) and the size of the whole template provides an exact measurement for the amount of cloth needed to cover the paper pattern, with a suitable allowance for turnings. The result of increased economy—making it possible to use the smallest pieces—and greater precision in pattern-making is important as a development in the traditional method of working. Although hexagon and diamond shapes only are illustrated, the same methods apply to all other geometrical shapes.

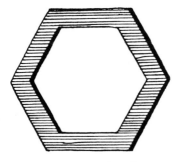

2 *Hexagon "A" Template,*
for materials

3 *Hexagon "B" Template, for papers*

4 *Diamond "A" Template*
for materials

5 *Diamond "B" Template*
for papers

PAPERS

There is no record of when papers came to be used in patchwork. It is probable that they were introduced with the first templates, but so far none has been found in work bearing a date earlier than 1770. It is also probable that papers were first used in the work done in upper-class houses; poor people did not write letters or if they did they did not receive them in large enough quantity to cut up for patchwork, as paper was an expensive commodity. It is popularly thought that "love letters" were used in patchwork pieces but this does not seem to be so; another (so far) unfounded legend is that "old wills" were also a source of supply. School copybooks have been used and often in work made by children; private letters were used in nearly all the nineteenth-century patchwork and some found in a Lincolnshire coverlet had been written by Tennyson to members of his family.

Date-stamps on envelopes, household accounts, letters and newspaper pieces can give a slight clue only to the date of the patchwork, but trade advertisements, sale bills and notices often contain enough information to be a guide as to the locality where the quilt was made. On pieces which are large enough, those cut from advertisement columns of newspapers give amusing and interesting information of happenings as long ago as the eighteenth century. Traditionally, papers are part of patchwork economy and not cut from sheets bought especially for the purpose; they should be firm enough to resist the folding of material at the edges but not as stiff as card, although they are often referred to as "cards". Anything thicker than brown paper makes work cumbersome and difficult to handle; thin card is occasionally used for very large patches. Good writing paper is the best standard for quality, but for quality, and convenience in having it kept neatly together, nothing can improve on the "Directors' Reports" issued to shareholders in prosperous companies. Excellent alternatives (not always acquired without some persuasion) are unwanted architectural and legal papers.

Good-quality paper patterns can be used several times if they are removed carefully from the completed work. It is necessary to remove papers from all patchwork which is intended to be washed. About sixty years ago some patchwork was made of silk and velvet and the papers "left in for warmth"; no doubt it was warm and also very heavy and quite unwashable.

NEEDLES

Needles should be comparatively fine, according to the materials. Patchwork seams need to be closely joined and this is done most effectively with a fine needle —size nine or ten is generally suitable. Some workers prefer "between" needles; being shorter than the ordinary "sharp", they work more quickly and are less liable to bend. It is often a source of pride if a favourite needle will last out the whole work, when it will have acquired a bend suited to the hand of the worker. Some quilters consider a needle is not in perfect condition until it is curved.

PINS

Pins for all processes of applied work and patchwork need to be smooth and sharp, most especially when the materials are cottons with a delicate finish, or silks. Steel dressmaking pins are suitable for most heavy kinds of materials, such as casement and linen, but they should not be left to rust in the pieces. Brass pins are most satisfactory; very short-length types, known as "Lill's" pins or "Lillikins" can be used in small patches and fine work, but brass lace pins are suitable for all kinds of material and are supplied in all grades.

THREAD

Linen sewing thread was used in all the early patchwork, some of it made from flax grown and spun in this country, and especially in some of the eastern counties and in Dorset. Dorset workers say they never use any but the local linen thread from Bridport. Fine linen thread can be used for herringbone-stitched appliqué and it is advisable to use it also for knotting or "tying" (p. 89). Linen and cotton appliqué is hemmed with cotton thread—sewing silk is more appropriate for loop-stitch or buttonholing; silk thread is used on light-weight silk materials but fine cotton is more suitable for heavy silks and satins and for velvet. All kinds of silk and metal threads are used for embroidery in *crazy work*; odds and ends from other work are often saved for the purpose.

Most cotton patchwork is sewn with cotton—white for all light-coloured pieces and black for the dark shades; for joining black or dark colours to white, a black thread is less noticeable than white. Thickness of thread varies according to the materials but sewing cottons numbering from 60 to 100 will suit most kinds.

SCISSORS

Two pairs of scissors are needed: one pair (very sharp) for cutting material and another for paper-cutting, as paper destroys the cutting edge of scissors. A razor blade (in a holder), or a seam-ripper, is better than scissors for undoing seams.

CHAPTER FOUR

GEOMETRICAL SHAPES AND PATTERNS

Geometrical shapes have been used to make patterns in most hand-work and are used as surface decorations in some kinds, such as embroidery, pottery and quilting, or are built into the fabric, as in weaving, mosaics or patchwork. Quilting and patchwork patterns are closely allied, and both are influenced by embroidery design; the connection between patchwork and embroidery is more marked in freehand appliqué than in the mosaic patterns. Patchwork and quilting patterns often come together in the same quilt, and there are many shapes which are mutual to both; the most common are the *square*, the *diamond* and the *shell* patterns; other mutual patterns are found in applied work.

Hexagon and *diamond* shapes are popular in English patchwork and most mosaic patterns are made from one or both of them. The *octagon* patch is not as

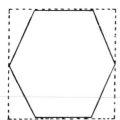

6 *Square converted into a hexagon by removing the corners*

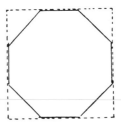

7 *Square converted into an octagon by removing the corners*

popular; it cannot be joined in a pattern without the addition of other shapes (generally squares) (p. 51) and this restricts the number of patterns which can be made from it. *Pentagons* must also be combined with other shapes to give a flat surface, as pentagonal patches only will not lie flat when joined. The addition of hexagons or diamonds (or both) is needed to make a quilt pattern (57). *Triangles*—whether long and narrow or short and broad—are in many traditional patterns and are found with and without the addition of other shapes, such as *squares*, *hexagons* and *diamonds*.

There is no standard measurement for any shape. The size of the patches is an individual choice and it varies in proportion to the size of the work—a quilt needing a comparatively large patch and a pincushion a correspondingly small one. Very early patchwork was made of square and rectangular pieces (*109*) and it is likely that all shapes with straight sides were made by folding and cutting squares of cloth. Curved patches would not be so shaped. A square folded edge to edge and cut will make two identical rectangles (*10*); if the fold is diagonal (from corner to corner) the two halves will be identical triangles (*33*). Subsequent

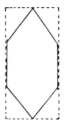

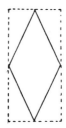

8 *Rectangles converted into long hexagons (Church Windows)*

9 *or long diamonds by removing the corners*

folding and refolding will make more, and smaller, squares, rectangles and triangles and so on. A square can also be converted into other shapes by folding down and removing triangular pieces from the four corners, and probably octagonal and hexagonal shapes were first arrived at in this way (*7, 6*); diamond and long

10 *Square folded into two rectangles*

hexagonal shapes were likewise contrived by applying the same process to rectangles (*9, 8*). Woven materials can be measured and cut by the line of the threads and many simple patterns are made this way.

Ordinary household objects, such as wine-glasses, saucers and coins, have been used for patterns with curving outlines; some shapes have retained the names of the things from which they were taken, such as the *wine-glass* and *pennies* in quilting. The key of a pair of ice skates was used for the template in one pattern illustrated (*175*). The semicircular *shell* or *scale* pattern is common to patchwork, quilting and embroidery—in the last two it is used as a background pattern. It is suggested that a variation of the shell with a slightly scalloped edge was taken from a biscuit or pastry cutter; it can be seen on the inner border of a silk quilt (*151*).

THE HEXAGON

The hexagon is the most popular shape in English patchwork and the patterns made from it—with or without other shapes—are characteristic of this country's work. As a six-sided shape, three variations are found in the patterns. The first is the *honeycomb* (*11*), so familiar that the popular picture of a "patchwork quilt" is one made from these equilateral hexagons: they are often called *honeycomb* quilts. The second—a *long hexagon* and generally called *church window* (*12*)—fulfils its description, as also does the *coffin* (*13*) but whereas this is used alone,

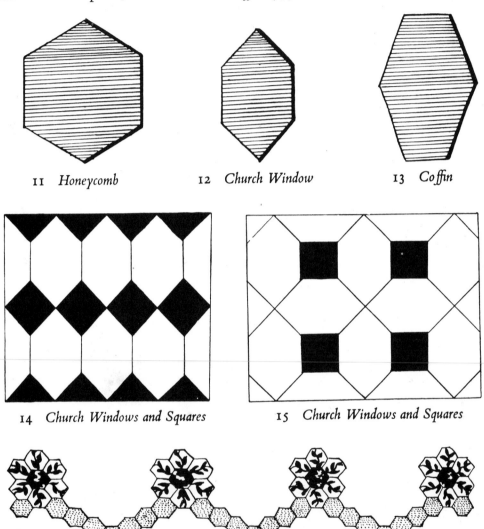

11 *Honeycomb*   12 *Church Window*   13 *Coffin*

14 *Church Windows and Squares*   15 *Church Windows and Squares*

16 *Border of rosettes linked by swags of coloured patches*

church windows are often combined with *squares*, or *octagons* or *rectangles*. The cope made in 1954 is made largely of *church windows* and they are contained in the Levens Hall quilt (*110*); the bed valance illustrated is of *coffins* only (*121*). Several names have been given locally to hexagon patches, especially in the West Country.

41

Mrs Hake discovered them disguised as "optigons", "octicians", and "sextains"[1]; they are also known as "sixes" and in many parts of the country are referred to as "squares".

Good border patterns are made from *honeycomb* pieces in *rosettes* and three are illustrated (*16, 17, 63*), as well as other arrangements in colour (*58, 59, 60*). *Star* patterns made from hexagons are common; one illustrated is typical

17 *Border of rosettes and single patches in colour contrasting with the background*

and is made of clear pink printed cottons, outlined with black patches patterned with emerald green (*141*). Diamond-shaped arrangements are found in many patterns (*147*) and hexagons are used with ingenuity to make the *hearts* and *kisses*, as well as initials, in the marriage coverlet illustrated (*124*). *Baskets* of hexagons in Mr White's coverlet "took a whole evening to figure out" (*175*).

THE DIAMOND

Diamond shapes vary according to the size of the apex angles and whether they are to be used with squares or hexagon patches. The *diamond* found in most

18 *Diamond or lozenge based on a hexagon*

patterns is that based on a hexagon (18); it is known also as a *lozenge*. The well-known *box* pattern is made from three diamonds in dark, medium and light shades of many colours, joined into a hexagonal shape and giving the three-dimensional effect of a cube, of which the top and two sides only can be seen (*19*). *Box* pattern has been used as a border (jacket) and as an all-over design from the beginning of the nineteenth century; about seventy years later curtains and cushions in silk were the essence of good taste and a cushion in an arrangement of blue, cream and white silk boxes is illustrated (*158*).

Many patterns are made from *diamonds* and *hexagons*; stars in *diamonds* are shown in a coverlet made otherwise of hexagons (*184*), and a design in black, grey and white was used for a cushion cover (*183*). Outlining or framing of *rosettes* with a single line of *diamonds* (*22*)

[1] *English Quilting*, p. 13.

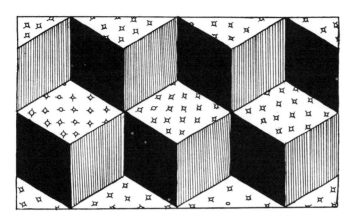

19   *Box Pattern*

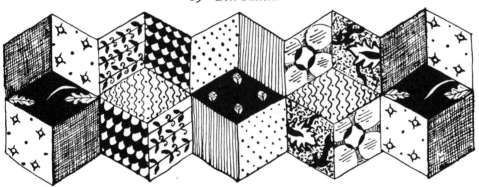

20   *A border pattern made from reversible boxes*

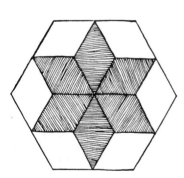

21   *Star pattern from diamonds*

22   *A pattern of diamonds and half-diamonds enclosing rosettes*

was done in eighteenth-century work and a coverlet in the Victoria and Albert Museum[1] shows this arrangement in coloured *rosettes* and dark-coloured *diamonds* on a white ground; the appliqué border is also outlined with lines of *diamond* patches. The chintz coverlet made by the Austen family (*122*) is made in diamonds of different sizes.

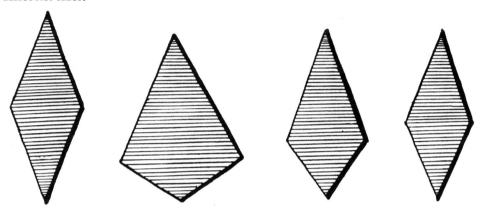

23   *Long diamond based*   24   *Diamonds which have become shortened at one end*
     on a square

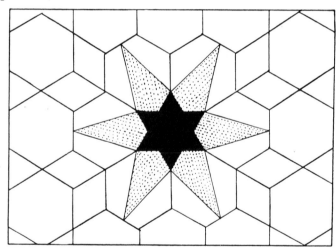

25   *Double star with other shapes taken from a nineteenth-century silk quilt*

The diamond shape which is based on a square is generally called the *long diamond* (*23*) and the *star* pattern it makes has eight points. A well-loved American "Star of Bethlehem" pattern is in the Victoria and Albert Museum collection of quilts, but the *long diamond* in English patterns is generally used with *squares* and *triangles*. It is found sometimes in cloth table-cover patterns and in some North

[1] *Notes on Applied Work and Patchwork*, Plate 12.

Country *star* quilts, as illustrated in *Traditional Quilting*, where it is used as a centre pattern. Smaller *stars* are also used in "block" patterns (see p. 55 for block quilts); an illustration of the *star* pattern in "blocks" is shown (*164*) and although

26   *Another version of a double star taken from the same quilt as in Fig. 25*

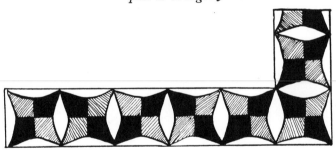

27   *A border and corner pattern in four-pointed stars and diamonds*

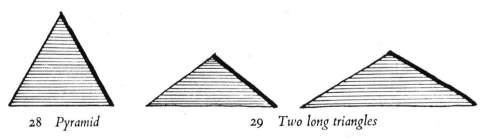

28 *Pyramid*   29 *Two long triangles*

in this quilt the stars are made from *squares* and *triangles*, the effect is the same as when the pattern is made with *long diamonds*.

Like many other shapes which began by being equilateral, diamonds have been altered and adapted from time to time, to make a special pattern (*24*); in some *star* patterns a second row of patches shortened at one apex, has been added to make a *double star* (*25, 26*). This kind of pattern is found under many names in American quilts but the English descriptions keep to *star*, *double star* or *treble star*. *Double stars* are made with either twelve or sixteen points. Shortened diamond patches are used for four-pointed *stars*, as shown in the pattern of the Cross on the chasuble (*155*) and in a border pattern (*27*).

THE TRIANGLE

Two kinds of triangle are used; one with a short base-line is known as the *half-diamond* or *pyramid* (*28*) and the other with a long base, usually called the *long*

30   *A border pattern made from pyramids known as Dog's Tooth*

31   *Zig-zag patterns for strip quilts in long triangles and pyramids*

triangle; *long triangles* (*29*) can be made either by dividing a square diagonally or by halving a diamond lengthwise.

Pyramids are used many times in borders when they usually make the *dog's tooth* pattern, as in the chair cover illustrated (*105*). North Country strip quilts in *zig-zag* (*173*) or *tree-everlasting* (*174*) patterns are often made in triangles of calicoes in two colours—pink and blue, lilac and yellow, red and white and so on. Cloth table-covers are made of *pyramid* arrangements and the shape clearly took the fancy of Private Thomas Walker, as he made his quilt from this shape (*152*).

Pyramids are often used with hexagons and diamonds.

46

Patterns made of *long triangles* are common in all-over designs, especially the *windmill*, which is one of the earliest and most persistent patterns. It is made from identical squares of different colours (light and dark shades, or one colour and

32   *Diagonal half-squares rejoined to make a different pattern*

33   *Squares of two colours cut and rejoined to make the windmill*

white) which are divided diagonally and rejoined, one piece of each colour, into squares (*33*). Border patterns are also made in this way (*35*), and the dog-tooth pattern is also popular for applied work quilts (*131, 140*). Another pattern is

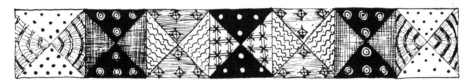

34   *A border pattern of triangles in opposite and matching pairs, known as "cotton reel"*

made when the triangles are rejoined in matching pairs, with the apex of each triangle meeting in the centre of each square (*34*). This pattern (sometimes called the *cotton-reel*) formed the border of a silk quilt made about 1780 and was an

35   *A border and corner pattern in long triangles*

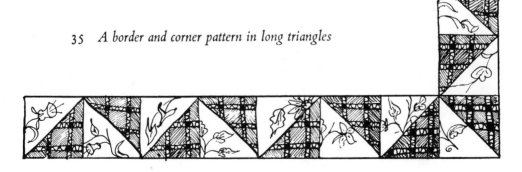

all-over pattern in an immense coverlet of cottons (appropriately made by six Miss Cottons) about 1790; the light and dark colours alternate in the adjoining

47

squares. The *basket* is another old and well-known pattern made from triangles; the baskets (*36*) are generally made separately and then applied to the squares in "block" quilts (*177*). It is made in one colour—red, green, pink, yellow or blue—and white as a rule, as the pattern depends on clear contrasts; the "handle" is a curved strip of material applied to the top of the "basket". When flowers are added in the *garden* and *flower basket* patterns they also are applied. The quilt illustrated has forty-two baskets which have been applied by machine-stitching; this is unusual and detracts a little from the appearance of the pattern. In Cumberland, the *basket* without the handle was known as the *sugarbowl* about seventy years ago. Many traditional *star* patterns are made from *long triangles* and *squares*; a straight-forward arrangement of two triangles joined to each corner of a square is illustrated (*55*) and with the addition of smaller triangles to the edges of the first star, the pattern becomes the *feathered star* (*178*). The illustrated quilt is made of pink zephyr gingham and white calico and the pattern is finished with a *saw-tooth* border.

36 *Basket pattern made from long triangles, with appliqué handle*

THE SQUARE

Quilts made from square patches only are rare—probably because the severe outline is not sufficiently inspiring and also it is remarkably difficult to make patches which are perfectly square. Chequered patterns in one colour and white are the most usual and red and white, or blue and white checks are used sometimes for *signature* quilts (see p. 55). A coverlet made entirely of *squares* about 1835 relies for its design on an arrangement of gradually shaded colour in succeeding borders.

Towards the end of the nineteenth century there was a vogue for pictorial designs, made in the manner of a cross-stitch sampler. The individual patches were rarely more than one inch square and sometimes less, and each patch was the equivalent of one square in cross-stitch canvas. A double-bed coverlet dated 1847 was made to represent a whole cross-stitch sampler, with the alphabet in rows in a centre panel and surrounding patterns of birds, animals and flowers. The pictures in the corridors and foyer of the dress circle of the Stratford Memorial Theatre are unique examples of this kind of pattern-making (*168*). The *American flag*—illustrated in *Traditional Quilting* (Plate 15) is popular in South Wales and the North Country and is made of brightly-coloured calico squares in a criss-

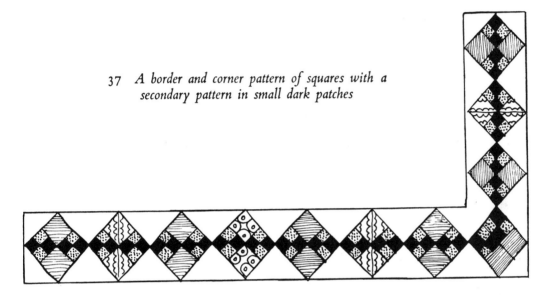

37 *A border and corner pattern of squares with a secondary pattern in small dark patches*

cross pattern on white. It is always done in one colour, mostly red, blue or pink, with a white ground. Border patterns made from squares are popular; many of them are used to surround centre panels (*125*, *130*) and several sizes of squares are contained in some of them, to make trim secondary patterns (*37*). North Country

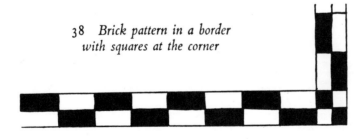

38 *Brick pattern in a border with squares at the corner*

strip quilts often have stripes of light and dark square patches alternating with others of plain calico or print; *squares* are inseparable from *octagons* in simple patterns made with this shape (*44*) and they are also used in patterns made with *church windows* (*14*, *15*) and rectangles (*38*).

49

THE RECTANGLE

Rectangular patches alone are not popular for pattern-making and have been limited to two or three traditional patterns. It is a shape which has been used mostly for the rougher kind of quilts made in districts where woollen cloth, homespun tweeds and flannel were manufactured; the trade patterns were easy to

39   *Adapted rectangular shape used with triangles in patchwork zig-zag border*

obtain and were joined without further shaping, in the brick-shaped pieces in which they were cut. Cotton trade patterns, identical in size and shape, were used to make *zig-zag* (*173*) and *brick*-pattern quilts (*146*). *Brick pattern* is always made with

40   *Rectangles set at an angle and used with triangles in a border pattern*

the patches arranged "hit-and-miss" fashion in light and dark colours; the muslin coverlet illustrated is in colours of pale blue, lilac and brown, but a more robust twentieth-century Weardale quilt is made of rose-red patterned cotton in the

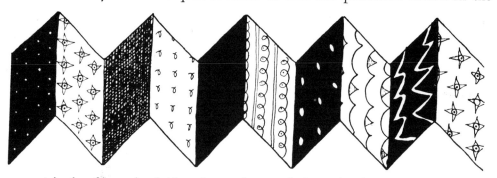

41   *A border of large rhomboid patches in alternate shades with a three-dimensional effect*

brick-wall pattern and is distinguished from *brick* pattern by unbleached calico "cement" between the *bricks* (*179*). The quilting pattern follows the patchwork.

Large rectangular pieces were often used in borders of quilts in which the design was made from smaller and geometrical pieces; narrow rectangular patches were often used to make border patterns for appliqué and patchwork coverlets.

50

The patterns were varied with patches set sometimes straight with the edge of the work (*38*), but more often arranged at an angle to give a serrated pattern (*40*). Short pieces of linen tape are used in some border patterns in a kind of zig-zag pattern, which is shown in two early coverlets (*114, 123*).

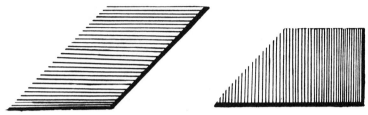

42   *Shapes adapted from the rectangle* (see Figs. *41* and *39*)

In common with other shapes, rectangles have been adapted to vary a pattern; one is a rhomboid shape (*42*) found in appliqué and patchwork *zig-zag* patterns and the other (*42*)—a little hard to describe—makes a similar pattern but is more often used with triangles in mosaic borders.

THE OCTAGON

Octagons need the addition of another shape to complete a pattern (*43*); it is not possible to join all eight sides of a patch to its nearest neighbours without leaving a square space on each alternate side. The space may be filled by one solid square

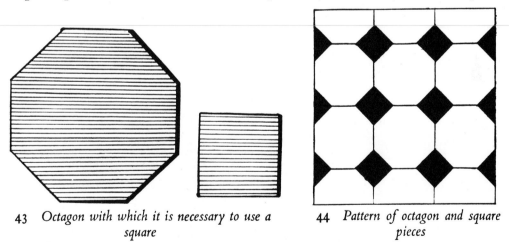

43   *Octagon with which it is necessary to use a square*

44   *Pattern of octagon and square pieces*

or a *square* made of two or four *triangles*. The *squares* are usually in one dominant colour such as scarlet, dark blue, black or brown and the *octagons* in a variety of colours. Large octagonal pieces are part of the pattern in the Levens Hall bed furnishings (*110*).

The best patterns show an attempt to group the patches into matching colours and this can be seen in the illustrated quilt (*161*), which was made in Devon and is typical of many patterns found in the south-western counties, especially Devon

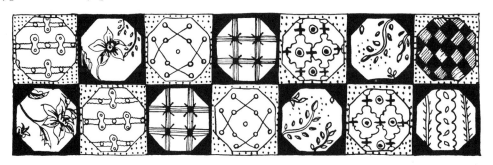

45   *A border pattern of applied octagon patches on squares*

and Somerset. It seems also to have been a local pattern in parts of Westmorland, where good quilts in red and white calico were made of it. It is used in mosaic border patterns and a border of applied octagons on squares is illustrated (*45*).

THE PENTAGON

It is not possible to make any flat patchwork from a number of equilateral pentagons joined together; twelve patches, when joined, result in a circular ball-like shape, to which it is not possible to add further pieces. At one time pincushions

46   *Equilateral pentagon*

47   *Pentagon used for box and star pattern*

made from these balls were used for workboxes or hanging ornaments in the parlour; they were usually made of silk or felt. Pentagons which are not equilateral were used to make the *box and star* pattern (*57*) when combined with a *hexagon* and *six diamonds*. A pincushion is also illustrated (*169*).

CHAPTER FIVE

GEOMETRICAL DESIGNS AND COLOUR

English patchwork patterns have remarkably few traditional names in contrast to the many hundreds which are found in American work. There are more variations of the basic patterns in American quilts and coverlets, but most of them seem to have developed from patterns which are in the earliest English tradition. It has already been shown that one pattern can acquire a number of names through a change of locality in America, but in England pattern names are more stable— the basic or descriptive name (with very few exceptions) being given to most

48   *Durham flower-basket*   49   *Devonshire flower-basket*

variations of the same design. A *plant-pot pattern* bears its original name whether it is made in Durham or Devon, a *windmill* or a *log-cabin* may be of Welsh or Wessex work, but in neither case does the maker or the locality impose another name, even though the pattern itself may acquire a "new look". Two *flower-basket* quilts (only partly geometrical), one made in Weardale, County Durham (*127*), and the other in Devon (*128*) are examples of this. The Durham pattern is in plain red, green and white calico; in the Devon quilt the colours are also red, green and white but the red and green cottons are patterned and the basket is more delicately made and the flowers and leaves show a greater skill in cutting and application.

A concession to change in the name of a pattern is that the colour is sometimes added. The *star* or *basket* patterns may become the *red star* or *pink star* or a *green basket* or *blue basket* and when appliqué flowers or fruit are added, the basket then becomes the *flower basket* or *cherry basket*.

Patterns of such great complexity were illustrated in the late nineteenth-century needlework instruction books that one can only suspect them as being inventions of the contributors and hope that many were still-born. Caulfeild's *Dictionary of Needlework* (published in 1882 and weighing nine-and-a-half pounds in the hand) contains a section under the heading of patchwork in which the patterns are reminiscent of those seen on the cheaper kinds of domestic linoleum. In 1885, Weldon's produced a popular series of instruction books called *Weldon's Practical Publications* (practical in more ways than one, as they were paper-backed and more easily handled than Caulfeild's dictionary), but the pattern illustrations for patchwork must have been a little confusing to the ladies who had followed Caulfeild, as some were inclined to be contradictory and names differed.

A number of patterns are peculiar to the North Country, where there is a strong tradition—and affection—for patchwork. The thrifty people of the moors and dales used their quilts as they were made, and as the patchwork wore out they were repatched, so that a seemingly new quilt really contained one or more earlier covers. Nothing of the slightest use was ever thrown away, but the owners of "old" quilts are very reluctant to show them and only with the greatest difficulty and the use of much diplomacy will any but the "best" quilt be brought out for a visitor to see; one often has to wait for washing day. Then it is a fine sight to walk through a dale village on a day in "quilt weather", with a fresh wind and bright sun, to see the washing lines full of *baskets, stars, feathers, plant-pots, American-flags* and *pincushions*, with as many as twelve quilts to a line.

Some of the Durham, Northumberland and Yorkshire patterns are found in some of the South Wales patchwork. This suggests the exchange of ideas and patterns between workers who lived in the mining districts in both countries where traditional quilting flourished, but the Welsh patchwork as a rule favours the comparatively large square or rectangular patches on which the quilting is easier to do and the stitches show to a better advantage. The custom of using large pieces in quilt borders was common in less skilled work and it was a matter of economy in time, work and material. The collected pieces were graded into sizes—the smallest were shaped into patches, the medium and larger sizes (which were often trade samples) were left as they were and joined simply by running together at the edges and the long strips were kept for the outer borders.

People in the quilting districts kept the pieces left over from the "plain" quilts and, together with odd dressmaking remnants, made them into patchwork for their "everyday" quilts. The quilting was considered more highly skilled than patchwork and some quilters could not (or would not) do the patchwork tops, but in the Southern counties the patchwork was more often considered to be the higher-grade work and the tops were "put out" to be quilted. It was usual in some homes where quilting was done for the patchwork to be made by the children and the grandmother.

The custom for *hearts* to be included in the patterns of marriage quilts is the same in quilting and patchwork. They are also found in cradle covers. All kinds of heart-shapes are used and they are usually cut out and applied, but occasionally heart-shapes are made in an arrangement of hexagons for marriage quilts and "kisses" are denoted by an ✗ arrangement of patches (*124*).

Signature quilts were made from patches about three inches in width (generally hexagons or squares) on which the names of the workers were embroidered, or in some cases written in indelible ink; they were a recognised way of raising money for charity about fifty years ago and patches were "sold" for about a shilling and the buyer's signature embroidered on the patch. "Hospital quilts" (also known as "Scripture quilts") were made in chequered patterns of red and white and texts written upon the squares, or scripture pictures outlined with marking ink. We are told that "they are much appreciated in hospitals and prove a great source of interest to the poor invalids". *Poor* invalids.

Generally speaking there are four accepted ways of building up geometric patterns in patchwork quilts but there are also the individual designs which, although traditional, fall into no special category. The "block" patterns are perhaps the simplest, although not the oldest method; next the striped or "strip" quilts. After that come the "all-over" patterns and then the type with a dominating central pattern, "framed" by a succession of patterned or plain borders.

The first three types—block, strip and all-over—are well-suited to the custom in which several people work together on a quilt, as sections can be made individually and joined when they are all completed.

BLOCK QUILTS

A "block" is made of a number of patches, in shapes that form a square when joined together. The simplest and most familiar pattern is the *windmill* (*165*, and diagram *50*); other types are shown in diagrams (*36, 53, 54, 55*) and quilts (*115, 159, 164, 177, 178*). Many appliqué patterns are made into blocks. There is no standard size for a block; some are as small as six inches square and others may be eighteen or twenty-four inches along each side. They are made singly until there are enough for the required size and then joined together just before the quilting is done.

The design of the quilt depends on the arrangement of the blocks, which are

usually made in two contrasting colours or in one colour and white. The patches are cut from the same templates in both colours and when the blocks are joined they are so arranged that the patches in adjoining squares are in contrast to one another. The simple patterns are the most effective. In those which contain the circular patterns, great skill is required in joining the edges on the wrong side without wrinkling the material.

The *pincushion* block pattern (*51, 159*) is known in Somerset as "Peter and Paul", which Mrs

50   *Windmill in mixed cotton prints*

Hake discovered when collecting material for her book on English quilting (Plate 28); the same pattern in America is "Orange Peel". *Steeple-chase* is a familiar "circle" pattern in the North Country (*52, 54*) and is usually made in pink and white, or red and

51   *Pincushion
block in two
colours*

52   *Steeplechase
block in two
colours*

white calico; the quartered circle in the pattern is known as the *jockey cap* in a Sussex silk coverlet and Elizabeth Jefferson used it in hers (*123*).

Pincushion, steeple-chase, windmill and similar blocks are joined side by side to make an unbroken pattern over the quilt, but an equally common arrangement has patchwork on every other block only and the alternate squares of plain material are given to quilting patterns (*164, 177, 178*) and the two *flower basket* quilts show applied patterns on alternate blocks. These quilts possess the quality

53   *Four two-colour blocks with colours interchanged. Jockey-cap pattern in the centre*

54   *Four two-colour blocks with colours interchanged*

of showing both patchwork and quilting to full advantage; in many all-patchwork quilts, the quilting pattern is confused or concealed.

Quilt patterns are also made from a number of squares each containing a

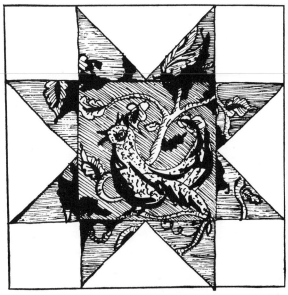

55   *Star block made from squares and long triangles*

pattern made from one or more differently shaped patches. In a late eighteenth-century coverlet (*115*) the squares show as many as sixty or more different patterns in appliqué or mosaic. The varied quality of the sewing suggests that it was made by a family and that children as well as grown-ups took a hand. Among many other designs made in the same way, *rosettes* are used as applied patterns (*63*); a typical coverlet (made about 1840) has ninety-four squares, each containing a *rosette*, which are joined by strips of matching cottons in a chequered pattern. Elizabeth Jefferson's patterns (*123*) also include squares with separate applied patterns made in the same method, as do scores of other designs.

STRIP QUILTS

A strip quilt is made, as the name suggests, with the pattern or colour running in bands or stripes from end to end. It is a distinctive type of pattern and is usually arranged with the stripes alternately plain and patterned. The patterned stripes consist of figured material or patchwork, but sometimes the patchwork alternates with printed cotton in small patterns. Striped patchwork quilts are still popular in the quilting districts and in the North are known as "strippy" quilts and the quilting is done in traditional running patterns along each strip[1].

The earliest strip-patterned patchwork is a coverlet said to have been made about 1780. It is made of printed cottons and chintzes and white calico and contains some eighteenth-century pieces but it has had a lot of repair, and cottons of various periods up to 1954 have been used to replace the worn pieces. The effect of light and dark stripes is achieved by the background colour in each of the two patterns, but the North Country 'strippies' are simpler and do not contain more than one pattern in the patchwork of a quilt. Two quilts illustrated were made in County Durham; one (*174*) is made of *long triangles* of pale lavender cotton set in yellow stripes (see fig. *56*, for detail) and the *zig-zag* pattern is in *bricks* of dark purple dress prints on a cream-buff ground (*173*). Striped quilts are made in a great variety of *zig-zag* patterns; many are made from large rectangles and even more show arrangements of *long triangles* or *pyramids* (*31*). A favourite with North Country workers is the *bellows* pattern, others prefer a pattern with *stars* in coloured print with wide stripes

56 *Diagram to show "Tree Everlasting" pattern*

[1] See also *Traditional Quilting*, M. FitzRandolph.

between the rows. The most popular colours are blue and pink, lilac and blue or lilac and cream, blue and creamy buff, or scarlet twill with lavender or buff-coloured prints.

The Welsh tradition in striped quilts is much the same as that in the North but the materials are more sombre in colour—purple, magenta and black are sometimes included in one quilt. One of the log-cabin patterns, the "V", is a strip pattern (*213*).

ALL-OVER QUILTS

A design in which geometrical shapes are joined in a continuous or repeating pattern is known as an "all-over" pattern. It is the commonest type and gained in popularity from about the middle of the nineteenth century. There is a very great variety of patterns—so great, in fact, that it is only possible to illustrate a few of the most typical. A book devoted to patchwork patterns would never come to an end.

Most of the English all-over patterns are made from the *honeycomb* hexagon. It is easy to make as well as being decorative. The single *rosette* has been the basis for hundreds of patterns and is often made from coloured patches and arranged singly all over a plain ground, with no other attempt at a pattern, except grouping the rosettes according to their colours. Colours are often disregarded and the arrangement is haphazard, but an attempt at a uniform pattern is made by the

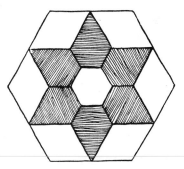

57   *Box and star from hexa-gon, pentagons and diamonds*

centre patch of each rosette being the same colour. The illustrated chair-seat cover is made in *rosettes* of eighteenth-century cottons (*105*) and a quilt shows a diamond-shaped arrangement in another all-over pattern of hexagons (*147*). A coverlet in which twenty-six thousand hexagons of cotton print are arranged in *stars* set in a ground of light stone colour was made about 1836 by an industrious lady in Norfolk—a Miss Lucy Brett. The cushion square mentioned earlier (*141*) was the work of the same artist and is believed to have been intended as part of the bedroom furnishing with the coverlet.

Diamond-shaped patches are made into all-over patterns of *stars*, as well as the well-known *box* pattern, but in many of these the rhythm of the pattern is lost unless the *boxes* are arranged properly. Everything depends on the effect of perspective being preserved and if a *box* is put in upside down the illusion is lost. Units or groups of *boxes* are used with hexagons in various patterns all of them

59

much like the chair-seat cover (*158*). Other combinations in all-over patterns include the coverlet mentioned earlier which can be seen in the Victoria and Albert Museum (p. 44) and the much-fancied *box and star* of Victorian days, made from a hexagon, pentagons and diamonds (*57*). Of the other quilts illustrated in this book, two are *brick* patterns (*146, 179*). A late-Victorian cushion cover shows one of the better instruction-book designs and is typical of its kind (*154*).

FRAMED QUILTS

The fourth type of quilt design has no traditional name in this country but the description "framed" may serve to classify a large number of quilts in which the characteristic of the design is a planned centre-piece surrounded by a series of borders or "frames". These patterns are not peculiar to any district and have been popular in poor as well as better class work. The centre panels are carried out in all-appliqué or all-geometric patterns or a combination of both or even a piece of printed cotton; the outline may be oval, round, rectangular or square and the squares are often put in diamond-wise.

The appliqué patterns are cut out from printed patterns or they may be formal shapes cut with the help of templates, generally sewn on to a plain foundation. A coverlet made about 1795 has plain calico borders decorated with floral appliqué (*114*); an early nineteenth-century pattern illustrates cut-out and template patterns (*140*); Elizabeth Jefferson's (*123*) and Mary Dickinson's (*126*) coverlets show framed centre panels which are the setting for their signatures and the dates of making. The borders in a coverlet in the Victoria and Albert Museum surround a square in *rosette* pattern. Mary Loyd's quilt is signed above and dated below the appliqué centre, but in Sally Eaton's coverlet the border patterns are more important than the centre. Specially printed centre panels (p. 30) were the height of patchwork fashion in the early years of the nineteenth century; two commemorative patterns are illustrated (*125*, and on the jacket) and many others have survived.

The outline of centre patterns made of geometrical patches is **often** that of the patch shape, as in Mr White's coverlet (*175*) but whatever the shape of the "frame" the quilt is always squared off at the corners to make it the standard shape for a bed.

COLOUR

The pattern of all patchwork depends equally on the colour and shape of the patches, and the proportion of colour in relation to the background makes up the general design. Unless colour contrasts are right no good pattern will emerge and the chief problem is to make an orderly arrangement from a large number of colours.

The simplest arrangement is the *rosette*; it is made from seven hexagons—one in the centre of six surrounding patches, which are usually of one colour. Enlarging the *rosette* by adding one row of another colour makes the *double rosette* and yet another, also different, makes the *treble rosette*. This is one of the earliest methods of colour planning (*106*).

Mixed colours are disposed of in rows of shaded patches in one of the *Ocean Wave* border patterns (*60*); two others are made from alternate light and dark wavy lines of colour (*58, 59*). The *shell* pattern can be made in many colours—the stronger and brighter the contrasts the better the pattern (see Chapter Six) *Strip* quilts are also a good way of using mixed colours, as also are the *log-cabin* and *crazy* types. Some colours have become traditionally associated with certain patterns. "Turkey" red was almost indispensable from 1850 onwards in cottage quilts made of dress and shirting cottons in *rosette* patterns; it is found in a large proportion of the North

58   *Ocean Wave in vertical wavy lines of alternate colours*

Country quilt patterns of one colour and white. Cotton dress prints in purple, mauve, blue, pink and buff-yellow are characteristic of late nineteenth-century patterns; black is inevitable in the silk patchwork of the same period, although it is said that it went out of fashion after Mrs Manning the murderess was hanged in a dress of black satin.

Unbleached calico has been used as a background for colour patterns since the earliest days of English patchwork but it is sadly lacking in present-day work.

The importance of the early patterns is the feeling for order and method in which the hundreds of coloured pieces are assembled in disciplined patterns, nearly all of them on a white ground. Geometrical patterns were made from groups of coloured patches, such as the *rosette* or the diamond shape illustrated *(147)* or the well defined *star* enclosing many mixed colours *(141)*. Some workers chose

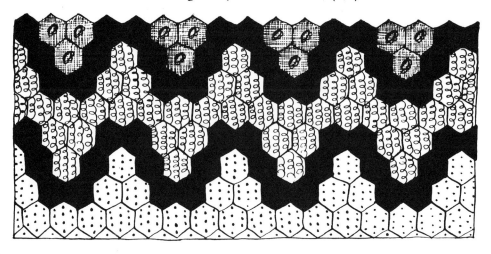

59 *Ocean Wave in horizontal wavy lines of alternate colours*

60 *An Ocean Wave border in shaded colours for the side of a quilt*

to select two or three colours only and others, as in the North Country interchange patterns, two colours, or one colour and white.

The best designs are those in which the proportion of pattern and space (i.e.

colour and background) is well-planned; the problem of an unplanned quilt has defeated many a well-intentioned beginner, judging by the sad evidence lying in so many attics and lumber-rooms. Proportion of colour is controlled by the number and size of the patches; bands or groups of concentrated colour will stand out more than single patches or thin stripes; certain colours in equal proportion will merge and the effect will be of one colour, as for instance when blue and yellow are combined closely the result will be near to green, or if red and white—the colour will appear to pale and resemble pink, and so on.

Many printed patterns contain a wide range of colours, and certain of them may be of more value to a design than others. These can be selected by the use of the "A" template, in whatever shape is being used, by laying the template on the material so that the desired part shows through the "window", and a complete picture of the finished patch will be shown (*193*).

Patchwork and winter evenings go together but the canny worker will choose her colours before the daylight goes.

CHAPTER SIX

OTHER TYPES OF PATTERNS

There are three types of patchwork which do not belong either to mosaic or applied work. The methods by which the pieces in them are joined together most nearly resemble those used in applied work, as the stitching is done on the face of the work. On the other hand, the patches are joined to each other and make up the fabric, so that the construction is more like geometric patchwork.

SHELL

Shell pattern is the only one of the three which has patches of a geometrical shape, i.e. a segment of a circle. No other shape can be used with it and it is always made in an all-over pattern. It has been familiar in quilting and embroidery designs for several centuries, where it is usually found as a background or "filling" pattern.

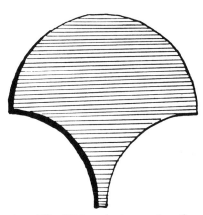

An embroidered satin quilt and pillow covers in the Victoria and Albert Museum show a *shell* ground to floral embroidery.[1] Two quilts illustrated in *Traditional Quilting* (Plates 9 and 49) show *shell* quilting among other patterns. It has never been greatly popular in patchwork because it is more difficult to carry out than the straight-sided geometrical shapes; the curved edges need careful handling and firmly woven materials are even more essential than in other kinds of patchwork (Appendix C, p. 176).

61   *The "B" or basic template for shell patchwork*

The pattern is known sometimes as *fish-scale*, as the patches are joined by overlapping them first, and they do then resemble the scales of a fish. The effect of a *shell* can be given by overlapping circular patches, but this is a clumsy method and wasteful of material; traditionally the pattern is made from patches which have been cut to the right shape (*199*). The design relies on the emphasis given to the elegant curving lines and in the best examples the shape is defined by the use of contrasting colours—either one colour and white (as in North Country quilts) or by a careful arrangement of light and dark shades of colour. Quilts of *shells* are rare. It seems that in American patchwork (where it is called the *Clamshell*) it

[1] *History of English Embroidery*, B. J. Morris, H.M. Stationery Office (Plate 22).

went out of fashion after 1800 and an early quilt said to have been made "before 1818" is illustrated in Ruth Finley's *Old Patchwork Quilts* which is made of white calico and dark blue cotton prints and shows the pattern at its best. There is little scope for variety in the arrangement of the patches, as the method of joining them demands that they be sewn together in straight rows, from side to side of the work. A usual pattern is one in which the colours of the patches alternate, light and dark, in the same row and the rows so arranged that the general effect is of diagonal or waving lines of colour.

No examples of *shell* patchwork have survived which are earlier than the last ten years of the eighteenth century, but it was an established pattern for quilting and embroidery long before then and possibly it may have been adapted to patchwork earlier than the present evidence suggests. A full-sized set of four bed curtains and valances made at the end of the eighteenth century are in the Victoria and Albert Museum (*113*). The patches are made from a variety of dress and small-patterned furnishing prints but there is little consistent pattern in their arrangement; the only definite pattern in the work is made by outlining groups of patches with a narrow green ribbon, hemmed on after the patchwork was made. The curtains are lined and each patch still retains the shell-shaped piece of linen over which the prints were sewn. Blocks of *shell* patches are seen in the "Sundial" quilt made in 1797 (*115*).

Little *shell* patchwork has been done in the last fifty years and only an occasional example is heard of now. A Northumberland quilt of Turkey and white twill made about 1890 has worn out and vanished; a coverlet in brightly coloured prints was sent to an exhibition in London in 1935 but it too seems to be lost. Since about 1950 some small pieces of *shell* work have been made and it may be that it will come back into fashion. Some contemporary work has been made in a different method from the usually accepted one; the pieces are inset and joined edge to edge as in geometrical patchwork but with slip-stitch instead of hemming for joining the patches. This gives a smoother result, but is an even more difficult process than the older surface-hemming, which is test enough for neat and even stitching.

LOG CABIN

The kind of patchwork which is known as *log-cabin* is unlike any other; no template is necessary, as the "patches" are measured strips of material which are sorted into light and dark shades of colour and the pattern depends wholly on the effect made by the order of their arrangement. The strips are worked into a square and the patterns which can be made are limited only by the number of ways in which the squares can be arranged. The diagram (*210*) shows a straight-forward arrangement of colour on two adjoining sides of a square, resulting in a diagonal dividing line. Two entirely different designs made from squares in this arrangement are illustrated (*157, 166*), whereas in the velvet coverlet (*167*) the light and dark colours were placed on opposite sides of the squares and produce such a different pattern that at first sight it seems hardly to have been made the same way.

These are only three examples of many scores of *log-cabin* patterns; innumerable different arrangements are possible, first of the strips in the squares and secondly of the finished squares which make the final design. In America each design has a separate name, but in this country they all are known as *log-cabin* irrespective of the arrangement; the pattern shown in the illustration (*166*) is identical with the American "straight furrow" and in common with the diamond *box pattern* it has a three-dimensional effect.

It is likely that *log-cabin* was one of the earliest kinds of patchwork. A Stirling-shire woman possesses a number of quilts made by her family from patterns which had been handed down from those used in quilts during the "Forty-Five". Some of them were made in squares of light and dark coloured cloth, but some in *log-cabin* patterns were made wholly of tweed and homespun woollen stuff.

The fact that each strip in *log-cabin* is sewn separately on to a strong foundation has made it more practical to use different kinds of material—such as silk, tweed and worsteds, satin and velvet—in the same work, as the strain is borne by the foundation. Most of the work is very rough, but nothing need be wasted, it is very warm and it can stand a reasonable amount of wear and washing. An early twentieth-century couvre-pied, made in Cumberland, consists of silk and satin brocades in lilac, pink and cream for the light colours and the contrasting strips are in black, dark blues, purple and reds. The good quality of the materials adds lustre to the work which is finely done. Ribbons were used in nearly every piece of *log-cabin* work; it is sometimes called *ribbon patchwork* and is referred to as such in Caulfeild's *Dictionary of Needlework*.

Whatever design is made, the patterns usually run to the edge of the coverlet, without any defining border or edge pattern. Sometimes one finds a pattern, similar to the "framed" quilts, in which the squares are arranged in a series of patterned borders. Other patterns are made so that the dark colours make diagonal or zig-zag shadows running across the work or, again, four squares are joined and the pattern treated in the same way as the *windmill* pattern (*33*).

Another pattern, in which the method of joining the pieces is the same as that for *log-cabin*, is a simple chevron arrangement of strips known as the "*V*" pattern. It consists of light and dark coloured materials stitched alternately in diagonal strips to narrow lengths of foundation material, such as calico, pillow ticking or sheeting. The pattern is made by joining the covered lengths so that the strips match in colour on each side of the join to make a "*V*" (*212, 213* and p. 185). This pattern seems only to have been done in Scotland and not later than the nineteenth century. The materials used were tweed and the quilts were lined and bound with Turkey red flannel. Air-holes were buttonholed in at intervals over the quilts, which were interlined with cotton wadding and described as being "far from cumbersome and easy to wash".

The "Pineapple" pattern is a variation, or perhaps more truly a complication, of the *log-cabin*. The strips are sewn in the same way, but in alternate light and dark colours and on every other journey round the square they are laid diagonally across the corners, instead of parallel with the sides (*211*). Each completed square contains four "half-pineapples" and the whole pattern does not emerge until the squares are joined. The illustrated coverlet (*176*) was made in Turkey red and white cotton by Miss Annie Thompson of Natland in Westmorland in 1920, and is a copy of one made by her mother in the late nineteenth century. There is another *pineapple* quilt in the Victoria and Albert Museum; it is of American work, and made from a variety of coloured dress prints.

CRAZY WORK

Crazy patchwork is said to be the earliest kind of patchwork of the last two hundred and fifty years, but there is no evidence to prove this in English patchwork. No examples of work exist, as far as is known, which were made before 1830 at the earliest and it is doubtful if it was popular much before the middle of the century. The essential economy of crazy work, like *log-cabin*, is that it is possible, though not advisable, to include many kinds of materials—woollens, silks, satins and velvets—in one piece of work. The scraps of material may be any shape so that every remnant may be of use and they are stitched to a foundation material which helps to bear the strain of wear and tear.

The use of elaborate embroidery is a characteristic of this kind of patchwork. Feather-stitching is used to cover the raw edges and preliminary stitching (see Appendix C) in the simplest examples, but where there was no real need for economy towards the end of the nineteenth century, *crazy work* became an excuse for doing more and more embroidery, until in some cases the patchwork itself became submerged in an encrustation of sequins, beads, ribbon-work, metallic braids and threads and embroidery silks. The stitches included a number of recognised embroidery stitches (*215*), but stars, hearts and other similar small patterns were also added. The patches of plain materials had flower sprays and figures worked on them often in raised patterns and the coverlets were finished with frills, or scalloped edges. Some of the more restrained work is charming, especially when the colours are well balanced, as in Jenny Jones' *crazy* coverlet (*163*).

Although the coverlets are usually referred to as *crazy* "quilts", it is virtually impossible to do quilting on this kind of work and there is no need for it; when it is lined, there is sufficient weight and warmth without the necessity for an interlining.

CHAPTER SEVEN

SHAPES AND DESIGNS IN APPLIED WORK

The applied work with which this book is concerned is of a more humble kind than its grand predecessors at Hardwick and elsewhere, but it has in no way come down in the world as regards skill and artistry. The earliest surviving coverlet dates from the end of the eighteenth century and the patterns are full of the life and colour found in the best tradition of appliqué. It seems at first only to have been done in the well-to-do houses.

Economy is the governing principle, as in mosaic patchwork and most of the patterns are sewn to a foundation material and not joined together by running or seaming. The patterns are in much greater variety than in geometric patchwork and the stitches, which are all made on the surface of the work, are included as part of the design (see Appendix D).

The word "appliqué" is used equally with the English term "applied work", and signifies the stitching of one textile on to another. In both words, the Latin derivation is *applicare*, "to fold" or "to fasten to"; the Concise Oxford Dictionary explains the verb "to apply" as—"to put close (to)", which is the more exact meaning of applied work. There are two kinds of appliqué in traditional patchwork: in one, the shapes are inlaid and so make up the fabric, as in mosaic; and in the other the shapes are attached to the surface of the main fabric, which is therefore—as the background—a part of the pattern.

INLAY

The inlaid work may be described as the connecting link between the true patchwork and appliqué. It has the construction of one and the pattern outlines of both, but it is more easily done in felted cloth or some similar material, as it is essential that the pieces do not fray. Two examples of inlaid work are described later in this chapter (p. 83) and notes on the methods used are given in Appendix D.

ONLAY

This is the most familiar kind of appliqué—that in which the patterns are laid on, and then stitched, to a foundation. It is sometimes known as "laid-work". It has almost unlimited possibilities for pattern-making, but it needs skill and more imagination in the planning than mosaic patchwork. Broadly speaking, there are two ways of making the individual shapes from which the designs are built up. One is with the use of templates, and the other is by cutting-out the patterns freehand, without any basic shape as a guide.

TEMPLATE PATTERNS

There are several sources from which template patterns are taken. First there are those in which the pieces are cut from geometrical patchwork templates.

The patches are made in the usual way (see Appendix B) and then (often in conjunction with other *un*-geometrical shapes) they are sewn to the background material. Applied geometrical shapes are often arranged and then joined in a group to make the centre pattern of a coverlet and three of these, all slightly different, are illustrated—an unusual *star* pattern in finely pointed *diamonds* (*104*), a nine-pointed *star* on the "Mary Dickinson" coverlet (*126*) and a pattern which is the forerunner of the present-day *Dresden plate* (*62*) in the middle of

62   *The Dresden Plate*

the "Sharman" coverlet design (*139*). A well-loved pattern for appliqué, found on both sides of the Atlantic, is the patchwork *basket* (*36*). Groups of hexagon or diamond patches are often sewn on to calico strip borders in *rosette* (*63*) or

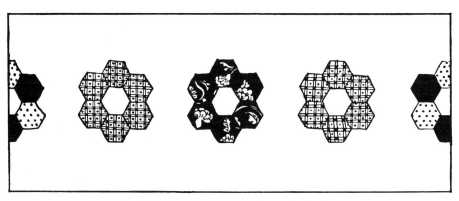

63   *Rosettes sewn to a calico strip border*

star patterns (*64*). Both are used as the "flowers" in some sprays of applied stems and leaves (*76, 136*).

Geometrical patches are often joined and applied in straight rows or patterns to make an outline which encloses or frames a part of the general design. It is a common arrangement on coverlets in which an elaborate centre panel is surrounded by succeeding borders of appliqué patterns separated by strips of patchwork. A good border pattern is illustrated in an appliqué coverlet (*104*) in

64   *A border of linked stars*

which rhomboid patches are joined in alternate light and dark colours for the two borders (see also *39, 41, 66*).

A second source of template shapes is the traditional quilting patterns, many of which are found in patchwork. Among the most familiar are the *rose, heart,*

65   *A border of linked squares*

true-lover's knot, feather, hammock, bee and *leaf* patterns, all of which are illustrated in *Traditional Quilting*. Patchwork adaptations of the *heart, feather* and *bee* patterns can be seen in a fine Northumberland calico quilt (*162*) where the centre *feathers* are alternately red and green, sewn to a white calico ground; the wide strip

66   *Appliqué zig-zag border made from rhomboids seen in Fig. 42*

borders are in the same alternating colours with white. The *hearts* indicate a marriage quilt and in this instance, in case there was any mistake about it, the applied patterns are quilted over and surrounded with the heart-shape in stitching.

The third source of inspiration comes from many of the homely objects about the house, although some of them suggest that the actual outline may have been traced or cut from a picture. *Plant-pots*, *vases* and *baskets* in all kinds of shapes, as well as *horns-of-plenty* (although hardly described as "homely objects") are used

67   *Leaf sprays made from elliptical patches*

68   *A Daisy pattern with the centre points covered*

69   *Tulips made from elliptical patches*

70   *Single Rose*

71   *Double Rose*

in designs where bunches or sprays of flowers appear to be arranged in them. A basic pattern was used when the patterns were repeated. Flower and leaf patterns whether natural or imaginary, are perhaps the most universally used. Plant and tree leaves can be recognised in many designs, especially oak, ash, ivy, sycamore and horse chestnut (*132*); an ordinary elliptical shape (perhaps taken from a laurel leaf) is one which was used equally well for a single leaf or a flower petal and

72   *Three Single Roses*

73   *Peonies*

74   *Carnations*

trailing sprays or flower heads could be made up from arrangements of a number of the separate pieces (*67, 131*). An elliptical template was used for some bell-shaped flowers and tulips (*69*), and some of the most successful were the daisy or sunflower patterns, when the patches were arranged in a circle with a round patch covering the points in the centre (*68*). Many flowers are cut from a single template but the flowers had more life in them when separate coloured patches were used.

A circular patch with a scalloped or serrated edge, to indicate the kind of

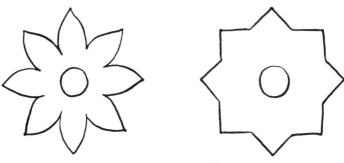

75   *Daisy or Sunflower*

flower that the worker had in mind, is found time and again in the cottage work; "double" flowers are shown by two layers of material. *Roses* (*70, 71, 72*) are much the same as those for *peony* patterns, but *peonies* are always more elaborate, with possibly three layers of coloured pieces or the addition of another shape

76   *A rosette as a flower with appliqué stems and leaves*

(*73*). *Carnations* are more closely serrated at the edges than *daisies* or *sunflowers* (*74, 75*); small circular or hexagonal "petals" arranged in a circle also make lively little patterns resembling flowers and seem to be found equally in mosaic and applied work (*134, 137*). It is likely that a basic shape was used for drawing each of the bird, animal and human figures (see p. 82) which are found in the rare and wholly delightful applied work coverlets of which one is illustrated (*145*), but the artist who was capable of work of this kind might well have cut out her patterns without the need for another tool than a pair of scissors. In some *bird* patterns the heads and wings are made from pieces or material, quite different from the body-work, and indicate a change of colour in plumage (*118*); a finely-cut leaf-pattern on the material may be arranged so that it covers the part of the body where a wing or tail should be and a small-patterned or spotted material used to indicate a speckled plumage and so on.

74

FREEHAND PATTERNS

Patterns which are cut without the aid of a template call for the most creative sense in the worker, as well as the greatest understanding of proportion, and an appreciation of space as a part of the pattern. They vary somewhat in degrees of

77　*A border of double bows*

excellence and the earliest which have survived reach a standard of perfection not found in work after about 1840.

The fashion for bows and ribbons in printed textile patterns came out in the

78　*A hammock border*

appliqué patterns; some were cut-outs from the printed patterns but generally they were made from odd pieces of plain or patterned materials. It is possible that templates were used for the border of double bows (a pattern used by Chippendale

79　*An elaborate hammock pattern*

for ormulu mounts) seen in the illustration of the coverlet probably made about 1790 (*104, 77*). Patterns such as this were made on the principle of paper-cutting and cut out from folded material, so that each side of the shape was identical

75

(*78, 79*). Narrow "ribbons", used for "tying" a spray or bouquet of flowers, were made from narrow strips of cotton and arranged in the shape of a bow. Typical *ribbon* and *bow* patterns are shown in two illustrated coverlets, one in the Victoria and Albert Museum (*140*) and another (owned by a descendant of the two sisters who made it) in which the bows are cut from a striped cotton giving additional elegance to the pattern (*139, 116*). Other illustrations show ribbon bows in the

80   *Two border patterns probably cut from templates or folded material*

patterns (*114, 129*) and the four which were made of a clear blue cotton in Mary Loyd's quilt (*81*), while lacking in elegance, are well-suited to the sturdy and colourful patchwork of dark green, brown, blue and rich yellow squares.

These illustrations show not only the typical *bow* patterns (popular from 1790 until 1840) but also the ways in which printed patterns, especially of leaves and flowers, were cut out and rearranged as designs for applied work. Sometimes a

  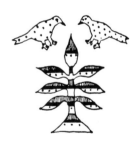

81   *Bow pattern from Mary Loyd's quilt*   82   *A Tree (variety unknown)*   83   *A Tree with alighting Birds*

whole design would be cut from a single piece of chintz and used as a centre pattern for a coverlet (*131, 143*); other patterns—separate flower-heads, leaves, birds and so on—would be cut from those on many different pieces of cotton and assembled to make another design. *Bowls* or *baskets of flowers* have always been first favourite for this (*122, 140*); game-birds (pheasants and partridges especially), doves, peacocks, parrots, birds of Paradise and many others were fashionable in the printed designs and so they were squeezed somehow or other into the appliqué also. In spite of the fact that many of the birds were too large for the under-sized twigs and branches on which they sat, the designs (and the birds) were well-balanced and lively (*83, 131, 143, 144, 145*). Although the floral chintzes were so desirable, they were not always easy to come by. The centre design might be made from a cut-out of a printed pattern, and the rest of the coverlet carried out in the more available and abundant dress materials. The character of a printed chintz pattern was often adapted to the striped and small-patterned dress prints, when they were used to represent the veining of a leaf or to emphasize the shape of a flower—the colours sometimes indicating green or autumn foliage.

GENERAL DESIGN

No pattern belongs to any particular part of the country, no two coverlets are ever alike, and although occasionally they have been intended for use as a pair, each has an individual character. There has been, however, an accepted formula for the fashion of the bed-covers. A centre design (very often floral) took up most of that part of the cover which lay on the top of the bed. This was nearly always enclosed in some sort of a border pattern, the outline of which varied and could be round, oval, square or rectangular; succeeding borders, with applied

84   *A border pattern from double rows of long triangles*

or patchwork patterns, completed the design. Whatever the combinations of technique, there could be no question of the work being unplanned. Geometrical quilts were sometimes allowed to grow of their own accord, but from the beginning, the designer of an appliqué coverlet had to be able to see the finished work in her mind's eye as it lay on the bed. She had to know also, more about the possibilities of her materials and what use could be made of them than was necessary for geometrical work.

The proportion of geometrical designs in appliqué varies considerably. In some work the whole of the design is carried out in appliqué, with only a border of patchwork; in these, the favourite patterns were those made from arrangements of triangular points and known as *dog's-tooth* (*30*) and *saw-tooth* (*85*) or a slanting *brick* pattern (*40*) or else one of the *zig-zags* made from triangles or rhomboids.

In all of them, much ingenuity was needed to negotiate the corner pattern neatly (*27, 35, 37, 38, 86*). The borders in other patterns were made alternately of appliqué and patchwork (*126*), or sometimes the appliqué may be sewn on to squares or other shapes which are part of the patchwork. The all-appliqué patterns were usually put on to coverlets, although the North Country adapted quilting patterns were applied to "blocks", which were later joined and quilted.

85   *A sawtooth border of long triangles in one colour and white*

The fashion for a day-time or top cover on the bed to be quilted went out from the early years of the nineteenth century until about 1830, and as the best of our surviving appliqué coverlets were made about this time, it is obvious why quilting was "not done" in both senses of the word. Later on (after 1830), when appliqué patterns were made of plainer or unpatterned materials, quilting appears with them and much of the stitching follows the outline of the applied pieces (*160*).

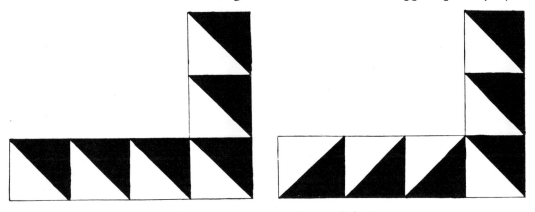

86   *Corner arrangements of sawtooth borders*

Good examples of quilting with applied work are also seen in the "Mary Loyd" quilt (*143*) and the Devon *flower-basket* (*128*); another can be seen in the quilted appliqué *plant-pot* pattern shown in *Traditional Quilting* (Plate 40), but on the whole, designs which include quilting come from the districts where traditional quilting was done. The quilts and coverlets which are illustrated have been chosen to show *typical* patterns or general design, although the applied work may not always be the most important part of that design. The earliest example which has come to light so far is also one of the best (*104*). The outer border below that with the double bows has an appliqué version of the quilting *hammock* pattern (*79*), rather more elaborate than a similar border in the Devonshire *flower-basket* quilt (*78*) and made about twenty years or so later. Other patterns show carnation and various daisy heads among sprays of leaves and flowers—eight slightly different

87   *A pattern of four hearts*

88   *A pattern of eight hearts*

plant-pots and four flower arrangements in two kinds of *vase* patterns; the centre square is lavishly adorned with *hearts* (*87, 88*), denoting a marriage coverlet, but nothing is known of its history. The patterns in early wood-block prints were sewn originally to the fine unbleached linen with loop-stitch with thin brown wool, but during many repairs (some as late as 1835), coloured silk and cotton thread have been added. The majority of the original "dark and shady" cotton prints of red, madder brown, purple and rusty black are lightened by twigged and sprigged patterns in rose, coral, indigo and pale blue, but many later prints are among them.

89   *Scissors and thimble applied to a square patch*

Patterns which are applied to geometrical shapes (*89*) and then joined to a mosaic pattern are shown in two coverlets (both signed and dated), one made in 1797 (*115*) and the other in 1811 (*123*). A centre pattern illustrated is outstanding for its pattern of cut-out Chinoiserie prints, herringbone-stitched to a calico ground, without a conventional "frame" (*129*). The rest of the ground is scattered with flower sprays and the border patterns contain flower sprays, butterflies and a flowing *ribbon* pattern. The herringbone stitch emphasises the lightness of the pattern and the work was probably intended to be quilted; it is a coverlet made by a

Durham woman who lived in South Wales and who doubtless used this stitch to give a smooth surface for ultimate quilting. Of two other appliqué coverlets illustrated, the "Isle of Wight quilt" is an example of a centre pattern (cut from the "partridge and plumtree" game-bird print) with an unusual surrounding "frame", the pieces of which obviously are cut from many different dress prints and hemmed to the background (*131*). Nothing is known now of the history or possible whereabouts of this beautiful piece of work; the only record is the photograph from which this illustration was taken and on the back of it was written "Isle of Wight quilt". No one now remembers it, and apparently it has vanished, but it is possible to see that it was lined and unquilted and so is not

90   *A bunch of flowers cut out from chintz and by templates*

91   *A flower pattern cut by templates*

properly a "quilt", and from the printed patterns it can be approximately dated about 1820. The second coverlet (*140*)—happily in the keeping of the Victoria and Albert Museum—has an oval centre frame of twisted ribbons set with sprays of flowers, surrounding an applied basket of flowers. The flower patterns are in colours of russet, brown and yellow and the leaves are cut from a green-patterned black cotton, most of them from templates. The *dog's-tooth* border pattern is cut from strips of cotton (black with red polka dots) folded and sewn as a Portuguese hem; it is said to have been made in 1825. This method of making a border was used in many of the appliqué designs around this time; it is seen again in a coverlet, finished about 1812, by Arabella Gwatkin of Herefordshire, who died in 1816.

The appliqué patterns in pink and brown chintz are buttonholed to the ground with brown silk thread.

Formal flower shapes are used in many of the *basket* and *flower-pot* patterns, from the early nineteenth century; similar quilts made in Devon and Durham have already been mentioned (p. 53) *peony* patterns are found also in Durham; *roses*, in sprays, have been found in Westmorland and in a "rambling" pattern in Wiltshire. *Baskets* without flowers are common all over the country; they are applied to square blocks, generally of white calico and the quilts made of alternate patterned and plain squares, with the *baskets* so placed that the "handles" are uppermost when the quilt hangs on each side of the bed. In a twentieth-century Weardale quilt with forty-two red and white *baskets*, the middle rows are set so that the handles lie towards the pillow end of the bed (*177*). In this quilt, as in most other *basket* quilts, the alternate white squares are quilted in the *feather circle* pattern.

Children's cot covers were made in appliqué and examples from as early as the eighteenth century are found. The patterns are taken from geometrical templates and quilting patterns and, considering their purpose, they are remarkable for their sombre colourings. *Hearts* are included in the designs and the baby's name is sometimes worked on the patches. A Leicestershire coverlet made towards the end of the eighteenth century at Barton-in-the-Beans has four verses of Isaac Watts's "Cradle Song" embroidered in cross-stitch on calico borders surrounding the centre square:

> Hush, my dear, lie still and slumber
>   Holy angels guard thy bed,
> Heavenly blessings without number
>   Gently falling on thy head.
>
> Sleep my babe, thy food and raiment,
>   House and home thy friends Provide,
> All without thy care or Payment,
>   All thy wants are well supplied.
>
> Soft and easy is thy cradle,
>   Coarse and hard thy Saviour lay
> When His Birthplace was a Stable
> And His softest bed was hay.
>
> How much better thou'rt attended
>   Than the Son of God could be
> When from heaven he descended,
>   And became a child like thee.

Thirty-six very small *hearts* are herringbone-stitched to the ground in blue, green and brown flower-printed cottons. *Hearts* are found in work done by children and in Elizabeth Jefferson's coverlet she applied her *heart* and her industry to good purpose, as the pattern is found in six borders of the design (*123*).

Pictorial patterns which include figures have never been as popular as others

92   *Heart patterns typical of children's work*

and they are not easy to find. The coverlet illustrated (*145*) is an exceptionally good piece of spontaneous work with familiar everyday objects, animals, birds and people in the life of the maker put in with a natural sense of design. All that is

93   *The Kitchen Tea-pot*   94   *The "best" Tea-pot*   95   *A Milk Jug*

known of it is that it was found in the effects of an old lady who died in 1922 and then acquired by its present owner[1]. It seems that it was planned by a family with a greatly varied collection of patterns such as tea-pots, jugs, baskets, socks, gloves,

96   *A Patchwork Basket*   97   *A Swan*   98   *The Barndoor Rooster*

shoes and dolls; swans, poultry, squirrels, horses, dogs, as well as jungle beasts and a host of other patterns, surrounding a floral panel. Another similar piece of

---

[1] Since this was written the coverlet has been presented to the Victoria and Albert Museum.

applied work (now lost sight of) has as its chef d'œuvre in the centre, a funeral hearse and horses cut from a black printed cotton—each horse with its head-plumes and others on top of the hearse.

The coverlet of inlaid work mentioned earlier has been described as "an example of unlearned artistry" (156). It was made by James Williams of Wrexham and took the ten years from 1842 to 1852 to complete. Two subjects were taken for the patterns—Biblical scenes and the engineering "wonders" of Wales in the nineteenth century. The Bible pictures include Jonah and the Whale, the Ark with a dove bearing an olive branch and the killing of Abel by Cain and in the dark sky over the scene, four strips of yellow felt, depicting the Wrath of God. The "wonders" include the Cefn Viaduct near Ruabon, shown with a train crossing over, and Telford's Menai Suspension Bridge, with a ship passing under and negotiating the currents of the Straits, which are shown by wavy lines of light and dark coloured cloth. It is not a beautiful piece of work but it is included

99   *A Squirrel*

100   *A Sock*

here as an example of inlay. Mr Williams no doubt found it a fruitful source of conversation with visiting admirers. Another piece of work in the same technique is a hanging kept at Overbecks near Salcombe; the centre of it consists of the royal Austrian coat-of-arms, with other coats of arms and pictures of famous buildings in Vienna in the borders, which include the Spanish riding school and two of the Lippanzer stallions.

The difference between work done in the "big house" and the cottage is clearer to distinguish in applied work than in true patchwork. This is not only in the use of chintzes, as against dress fabrics, but the upper-class work was of a more leisured kind, with finer patterns and detailed planning which is seen only in work for which time can be set aside, and the need is not urgent. A good deal of it has been preserved, and this was no doubt because of the value which was put upon the chintzes in the height of their fashion. The cottage work is simpler and the dress prints are better suited to a less sophisticated kind of pattern. Both types have one thing in common, in that calico, whether white or unbleached, was used for nearly all appliqué coverlets; other alternatives were white or unbleached twill, or cotton.

CHAPTER EIGHT

LINING AND FINISHING

However well-made the patchwork of a quilt or coverlet may be, the lining and finishing of the work have the last word in the length of its life and good appearance. The lining gives support to the fabric, as well as protecting the back of the patchwork and containing the interlining where this is included. It must be attached securely and at the same time it may be considered as a part of the design, by the methods in which this work is done.

There are two traditional ways in which linings are fastened to the tops of patchwork quilts. Quilting is probably the oldest method and when this is done the pattern of the stitching always supplements the surface pattern and in some cases even dominates the patchwork, as in the traditional quilting designs which have become almost inseparable from it. In the less decorative but no less efficient method of "tying" or "knotting", there is also scope for a limited addition to the pattern. The work of attaching the lining is carried out in two stages; the first consists of stitching from the surface of the work through to the back by one of the two methods mentioned; and the second is the final neatening of the edges by binding, piping or running them together to complete the joining of the top and lining. The addition of a fringe or a frill to the edges has been fashionable from time to time.

REMOVING THE PAPERS

The paper patterns are removed from all work which is likely to be washed and this is done before the lining is added. In certain things (such as needlebooks) in which a cardboard stiffening is included, there is no possibility of washing being done and papers are usually left in. All that is necessary to remove them, is to draw the tackings from each patch and lift out the loosened paper. Those which are undamaged are saved and used again several times.

LINING

The fabric of the lining (or backing) must be appropriate to the materials which make up the patchwork and be firm enough to hold the top securely, but not so heavy that it will pull away in use. Appliqué coverlets are rarely lined unless some part of them is made of patchwork; in this case the raw edges on the wrong side of the patches need the protection of a backing material and then the coverlet is lined throughout. Some patchwork has been left without a lining intentionally. Illustrated examples of this are the "Sally Eaton" coverlet (*124*) in which the hexagonal patches appear to have been made without papers but the tacking stitches on the hems remain; they cannot be seen from the front of the work and were evidently meant to prevent the corners from becoming unfolded. This method was successful as the back is still neat and tidy, in spite of the coverlet having had a certain amount of use. Another coverlet without a lining (*114*) has had the tackings removed and the hems on the wrong side are still in good condition after a hundred and sixty years but the coverlet has not been used. A lining was never intended, as the edges are finished with a binding.

Numerous coverlets which were probably intended to remain unlined now have backings of later periods attached. It is impossible to know whether these were replacements of original linings or later additions to previously unlined work, in attempts to preserve it. Loose covers for chair-seats and cushion covers made in mosaic patterns are generally unlined, but sometimes a piece of muslin or thin scrim is stitched lightly to the back of the patches. Curtains are lined with thin calico or sateen, which is attached at the top and sides only. Dust-sheets were made from rough and unlined patchwork, generally large trade patterns, sewn together especially for the purpose; a Somerset woman remembers unlined patchwork covers being so made for the spring mattresses on the beds. Quilt linings are often made from large square and rectangular shapes of cotton print, gingham, shirting or chintz, which were run together at the edges and joined into strips; the strips were then sewn to fit the back of the quilt. Occasionally a patchwork lining had a definite pattern, although it was a secondary and less decorative affair than the top. The silk coverlet illustrated (*151*) has a particularly good reverse side for the lining.

Silk, or silk and velvet, patchwork, was usually lined with sateen, especially if the work was of any size; in smaller objects, such as bags and Victorian reticules, satin was more often used. Satin is also found on small coverlets and couvre-pieds, when it is generally black in colour, doubtless for economy's sake. The colours of sateen linings were usually grey, fawn or drab yellow, as well as black. Patterned cottons, such as "Paisley" designs and sprigged chintzes are included in traditional lining materials but the nature of some especially stiffened chintz linings made quilting impossible and they are used only for curtains and unquilted coverlets. The majority of all linings are made from white or unbleached calico, cotton, linen or twill and sateen; cotton poplin has been used in many of the twentieth-century quilts and coverlets. In keeping with the general economy of the work, and because of their cheapness, all these materials except poplin and sateen are unbleached and linings made from them in lengths bought especially for the purpose. Repaired household sheets, as well as other used and sufficiently large pieces of material are suitable for linings.

Linen backings are a feature of many quilts found in the south-western counties of Somerset and Dorset; the weaving and thread is somewhat rough and although at first unbleached, it has become soft and white with use. Most linings are composed of two or more widths of material according to the size of the patchwork top and in cases of obvious economy as many as four or six large squares have been joined. The joining has usually been done by hand but the lining seams in recent work are sometimes stitched by machine. Years of wear will test the endurance of all stitching and although hand-sewing is preferable on the finest cottons, machine-stitching is useful for long seams which need a strong join. All seams are better if kept to a minimum when quilting is to be done; unevenness in the materials adds to the difficulties of quilting on patchwork in any case and when a large number of seams is unavoidable, tying or knotting is a good alternative (p. 89).

INTERLINING

The presence of an interlining in a patchwork bed-cover transforms a solely decorative coverlet into one which becomes valuable for its warmth also. The cheapest sort of padding is cast-off woollen clothing, in which the seams have been unpicked and pressed flat, but it is also very heavy if more than two thicknesses are used. In the past this kind of padding was used in the poorest households only and even woollen stockings were put in, so that nothing was wasted. The cloth patchwork of South Wales contains this kind of padding; a recently made "stuff" quilt in Yorkshire is of new tailor's patterns, interlined with layers of used woollen clothing and backed with strong unbleached calico; it takes a week to dry and needs two people to lift it on to the clothes line. Even when dry and in use, it is heavy enough to discourage easy getting-up in the mornings but it is typical of many hundreds of "stuff" quilts still in use.

Partly-worn blankets have made many a good interlining. In sheep-farming districts, some of these have been woven at home and "finished up behind the patchwork". Pieces of thin blanket can be joined carefully to avoid thick seams and are found in quilts made from cotton dress prints for the last hundred years. Some of the more recent ones are thinly padded with flannel and flannelette and in South Wales those containing lengths of Welsh flannel are put by for half of the year and used as "summer quilts" only.

Sheep's wool is probably the earliest kind of padding for traditional quilts in this country. It has always been comparatively plentiful in sheep-farming districts and a good deal can be had for the collecting from hedgerows, barbed-wire fences and briar patches. After shearing time, odd clippings and spoiled parts of the fleeces can be taken and washed free from grease and dirt until they are clean enough to be carded and used in patchwork quilts. Nowadays there seems to be little difficulty in obtaining wool from farms at the current prices; unwashed and uncarded, the price is about six shillings a pound. Supplies of hedgerow wool can be supplemented in this way and where there are local mills, it is often possible to buy "seconds" (second quality) by the pound, washed and ready for carding.

Clean carded wool can also be bought ready for use and the amount needed depends on the size of the quilt and the thickness of padding preferred by the maker. The usual amount required for a single-bed quilt is from one and a quarter to one and three-quarter pounds and for a full-size quilt to fit a double bed from two to four pounds would be used. Cotton-wool and cotton-wadding have been used in nearly all North Country quilts since about 1830, but in South Wales sheep's wool was used for most of the padding, from the evidence in patchwork quilts made there. All sheep's wool needs carefully cleaning for interlining; if it is not free of the natural oil, small brownish marks will appear on the outer covers of the quilt.

Paper has been recommended as a padding material; Caulfeild's *Dictionary of Needlework* states that: "Quilts of paper are much used for charitable purposes, as the material of which they are made is very susceptible to atmospheric influences and promotes warmth by retaining the heat." Instructions then follow for filling a number of chintz bags and setting them together "as in patchwork". This procedure may explain the reason why, when Oliver Twist's mother turned in her workhouse bed, to catch a glimpse of her newly-born child ("Let me see him and die"), we read that "the patchwork quilt which was carelessly flung over the iron bedstead *rustled*". Clearly a "charitable quilt" had found its way into the workhouse.

QUILTING

The two traditional methods, by which the three layers of an interlined quilt are stitched together and so kept in place, are quilting and "tying" or "knotting", in which the work is literally tied together. Quilting is undoubtedly the perfect complement to a well-designed patchwork quilt but technical knowledge as well as skill and equipment is necessary to carry it out.

The quilting tradition is as ancient as that of any other kind of needlework in this country and it is most familiar now in its association with the making of bed coverings. We know that it joined forces with patchwork, at least as early as the beginning of the eighteenth century, as shown by the "Levens Hall" quilt (1708), where the quilting is carried out in a red thread. There is a strong quilting association with patchwork in many parts of the country, particularly in the North, South Wales and the south-western counties of England. It was a common custom in districts where quilting was a means of earning a livelihood for the professional workers to be commissioned to quilt patchwork tops made by those who could not quilt. The professionals would rarely make a patchwork top for a quilt, unless it was for themselves or their families; this was especially so with the women who combined their quilting with the business of village dressmaker, but it was a generally understood thing that the patchwork should be provided by the customer who required the quilting to be done.

The rates of pay varied in different parts of the country. It cost from sixpence to a shilling to have the patchwork quilted in South Wales, although some well-known quilters received as much as five shillings. In Cornwall three shillings and sixpence was "a fair price" but some workers received ten, fifteen or twenty shillings; a worker in North Devon charged her neighbours three shillings and sixpence. In the North, "Quilt Clubs" were run, in which the work was done and charged for on an instalment system—weekly payments were made while the quilting was being done. During a revival of quilting as a home industry, from 1929 until 1939,[1] a standard rate of two shillings and sixpence the square foot was paid for fine work, which gave the quilter an approximate amount of three pounds sixteen shillings for her work on a quilt.

Quilting is a craft on its own, but no book on patchwork would be complete without its inclusion, both in the making-up of the patchwork tops (as in this chapter) and in the part it plays in patchwork patterns. In spite of this association it is not possible to give detailed instructions in the technique here, but only the general requirements necessary for completing a patchwork quilt.

To do the work successfully it is necessary to have a proper quilting frame; a rough method sometimes adopted is to spread the work on the floor and run the layers together as they lie in position, with diagonal lines of stitching, but this is not to be recommended. It may well be that the size of a quilting frame is a handicap; one of medium size measures approximately five feet six inches long and three feet wide, when set up for working—not an easy thing to accommodate in any but a large room. Some American workers use a large circular frame, similar to those used in embroidery, but this entails doing the quilting in small sections, while holding the work on the knee; it is not an easy method. For those who have no knowledge of the correct technique, a certain amount of practical instruction will go a long way and experience will do the rest.

[1] *Traditional Quilting.*

In districts which have an established quilting tradition, the patchwork pieces are comparatively large and the designs simple, so that the quilting will show to the best advantage. Many of the quilts are made in blocks, alternately patchwork (or appliqué) and plain, with the most elaborate quilting done on the plain squares. In a number of the North Country patterns made from plain self-coloured and white calicoes, the quilting patterns are dictated by the outlines of the patchwork (*160*); in the strippy quilts the long flowing patterns such as *running feather, twist* and so on, are found on the plain stripes, whereas the patchwork is quilted with one of the plainer background patterns such as *diamond*.

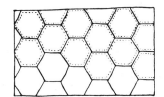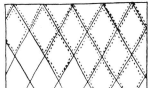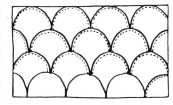

101   *Quilting stitches following the shape of each patch*

A pattern of double diagonal lines, quilted on a patchwork pattern made by Dorcas Jolly in Westmorland about 1850, was called the *matrimony* pattern.

The unskilled quilting patterns in geometrical patchwork are those which follow the outline of the patches, so that the effect on the back of the work is of an all-over pattern, such as *honeycomb, diamond, shell* or whatever other shape the patches may be (*101*). It is a simple method and may be done without a quilting frame, as long as the layers of material are thoroughly tacked first; a good way of doing this is described in the method of preparation for tying.

TYING OR KNOTTING

The process of tying a quilt or coverlet can be done efficiently only if the two or three layers of material are first tacked together, and then if the "ties" are spaced evenly over the surface of the work at short intervals.

To prepare the work it is necessary to spread the two (or three if an interlining is being used) layers of the work fully and smoothly on a large table or on the floor; while they are in this position, tacking stitches are run in several parallel lines—first from end to end and then from side to side of the quilt (*102*). Each line of stitching along the length begins from the top and is taken towards the opposite end; likewise the crossing lines begin each time from the same side. Tacking always from the same direction is a safeguard against wrinkling, which is likely to happen without this precaution. It will be found more satisfactory to use a woven interlining in "tied" quilts, such as worn blanket or flannel; sheep's wool or cotton wool is not held securely enough.

When the tacking is completed, the tying is done, if possible, without moving the quilt from the position in which it was tacked. A linen thread is used and the "ties" consist of single backstitches placed at regular intervals over the surface

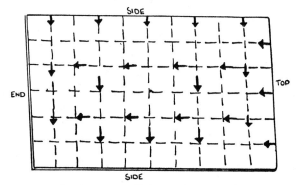

102   *The direction of the tacking stitches in*
preparation for tying a coverlet

of the work; these may be in white or natural-coloured thread, or a coloured thread to match or contrast with the colour of the patches may be used.

To make the ties or knots:

(i) Make a stitch about one-eighth of an inch in length through all the thicknesses of the quilt (*103/1*).

(ii) Draw the thread through the stitch until about two inches remain.

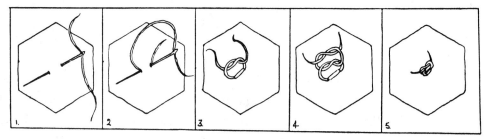

103   *Five stages of making a knot for tying*

(iii) Make a back-stitch in the identical place of the first and draw up the thread firmly but without puckering the material (*103/2*).

(iv) Knot the ends firmly, making a reef-knot (*103/3* and *4*).

(v) Make the knot firm and cut off both ends of the thread so that they are the same length—about one-third of an inch (*103/5*).

104　*A fine linen marriage coverlet with appliqué patterns of early wood–block cotton prints in red, pink, rose, blue and white patterns on dark grounds of purple, madder brown or black. c. 1790*

106 *Detail of fig. 105. Showing eighteenth-century wood-block cotton prints and floral patterns drawn in black, filled with pencilled colour. c. 1785*

105 *Chair-seat cover with white ground and coloured rosettes in shades of pink, rose, blue, buff, black and brown. The border of pyramids is finished with a linen fringe*

The distance between one stitch and the next, in any direction, should not be more than six inches and a space of four inches will reduce the strain on the patches and make the work firmer; the patchwork pattern can be used to regulate the spaces. For example, if the patches are hexagons the ties can be made on every third or fourth patch in every direction, according to its size—large patches should be tied on every third one and smaller sizes on every fourth patch (*107*).

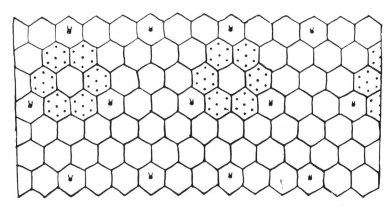

107   *Knots or ties made on every fourth hexagon patch*

Tied quilts are not common, although a number finished in this way in recent years suggest that the method is gaining favour. The "stobbed" quilts made during the last century in County Durham were held together by this method and Florence Peto mentions an eighteenth-century appliqué coverlet (taken to America by a young bride) which was eventually finished by another worker who, "with an eye to a short cut, fastened the layers together with blue and white cotton thread tied in small bows".[1]

FINISHING THE EDGES

After the quilting or tying has been completed, the uneven patches in the last rows are turned in to straighten the edges of the patchwork, so that it may be attached to the lining. There are several traditional ways of finishing a quilt; fringes were fashionable for the first fifty years of the 1800s—those on cotton coverlets were made of linen thread and the heavy silk fringes of later quilts were usually yellow. Caulfeild (1882) recommends "ball fringes" (then being commercially produced) for "mats or handkerchief sachets" and they are found also on cushion and mantel-covers, but not apparently on quilts or coverlets. An unusual finish to a *log-cabin* couvre-pieds is a four-inch border of hand-made

[1] *American Quilts and Coverlets*, Plate 6b.

string lace, with a woven pattern of red, blue and metal threads (*157*). Gathered or pleated frills finish off innumerable quilts from about 1850 onwards; they are found in abundance on cushion covers also, particularly on those made of *crazy work*, when they were generally of black or yellow satin or sateen. A cotton coverlet made about 1840 has a frill of pink and white candy-striped cotton; scalloped frills were fashionable in the early 1900s and Mr White intended his work "to have a flounce put on it" (*175*).

One of the most usual finishes is a binding which covers the edges of patchwork and lining. Many early coverlets are bound with strong fine braid made of silk, linen or cotton; the colour is nearly always dark green or white, royal or dark blue, plum-colour or red. Wide linen tape, white, black or unbleached, was

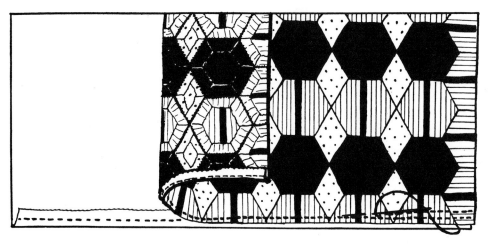

108 *A method of finishing by turning in the edges of the lining and patchwork top and running them together*

also used. Braids or tape are put on straight and mitred at the corners; binding with cross-cut strips of material does not seem to have been a means of finishing before about 1850 and any which appears in earlier work has been added as a repair or to strengthen the edges. Covered piping cord is found on quilts of all periods; it is undoubtedly the finish which best preserves the edges from wear and tear and it can be replaced when worn, with little trouble. The covering of the cord is usually strips of material, cut on the cross, and the colour of it is in keeping with the general scheme of the quilt. Another means of covering is by joining all left-over patches from the work into a single row, so that they form a strip long and wide enough for the purpose. The covering must fit the cord closely and the sewing done as near to the cord as possible, with *firm stitches*, not lightly tacked in, as is sometimes the case. A good method of securing the covered cord between the edges of the work is to hem it on each side, rather than to run it on one side and hem it the other. One of the accepted finishes for traditional quilting is that in which the edges of lining and top are run together with two parallel lines of stitching (*108*). It is found in many of the earlier patchwork quilts and is a method used then even more than the piping cord edge. Another way in which patchwork may be finished is that in which the last row of patches is turned over to the back of the work and hemmed down to the lining, the papers having been removed previously. An alternative but similar method is to fold over the lining to the front and hem down the folded edge to the patchwork.

CHAPTER NINE

THE EIGHTEENTH CENTURY

The gay and lively influence of the "new" coloured cottons, so much in favour at the end of the seventeenth century, can be seen in most of the patchwork which was made during the eighteenth and early part of the nineteenth centuries. The colours and patterns were irresistible; their fastness in washing and the hard-wearing quality of the calico and linen well repaid the care and planning which went into the work, and are the reasons why so much more cotton patchwork than any other kind has survived.

The earliest-known English patchwork was made in 1708 at Levens Hall—the "pale house with its topiary gardens"—which stands not far from Kendal, in Westmorland (*110*). The work consists of a quilt and bed hangings made from pieces of imported Indian calicoes and, so far as is known, it is the only patchwork in these materials which now remains. It is not known who made the hangings but it is presumed that the second wife of Colonel Sir James Grahme (the owner of Levens at that time), helped by her step-daughters and women of the household, patched and quilted these historic furnishings. The background patches are white and the coloured *octagon*, *church window* and cruciform shapes are repeated singly, at intervals in the ground, on quilt and curtains alike. The colours—in shades of red and blue—are still clear, although mellowed with age and, with the exception of a few worn places, the fabric is still intact. The patterns, both large and small, are characteristic of Indian work. Several patches have been made up of a number of smaller pieces and this joining of small fragments of especially scarce or highly-prized materials is a common practice in patchwork of all periods and is in the accepted tradition. The whole work is quilted with an all-over *diamond* pattern in a red thread and in this, as well as the patchwork, there is nothing of the rough or elementary economy which might be expected in any kind of work still in its infancy. This infant had passed its teething troubles and suggests that earlier work had been done; the only indication that some of the work might have been at all experimental is that some patches seem to have been adapted to fill in odd spaces, but even these are made by an expert needlewoman.

Other examples of early eighteenth-century patchwork are hard to find; a small fragment of hexagonal silk pieces, now fragile and worn, is reputed to be of the "Queen Anne" period, but no record of it exists. By the early 1720s patchwork had become a common enough occupation to be used as "copy" in a work of fiction; Jonathan Swift in *Gulliver's Travels* (published in 1726) remarks

109 *Part of a silk hanging made from votive fragments during the
sixth to ninth centuries*

110 *Detail of a quilt at Levens Hall, Westmorland, containing imported Indian
painted calicoes in shades of red and blue. c. 1708*

111 *Part of a strip coverlet of cotton dress and furnishing prints of many colours with brown predominating. c. 1780*

112 *Cushion square with long triangles in the windmill centre and on the borders, in faded pink and brown cottons. Calico border embroidered with black chain-stitch. Dated 1786*

113 Part of a set of bed hangings of shell pattern in many coloured cotton block prints, with sections outlined in green braid. Late eighteenth century

114 A coverlet in cotton prints with dark blues and greens predominating. The centre of appliqué and borders of patchwork and patterns in linen tape. c. 1795

115 *A cotton coverlet in a great variety of geometric and appliqué patterns, including a sundial in the
centre and two hemispheres and maps of England and Scotland in the corners. Dated 1797*

that Gulliver's clothes, measured and fitted by three hundred Lilliputian tailors, "looked like the patchwork made by the ladies in England, only that mine were all of a colour". There does not seem to be any other record, nor any traditional work, still in existence from that time, which is remarkable considering that there must have been a sufficient supply of pieces of silk and cotton for work which we know to have been established.

There is good reason to believe that woollen stuffs were used for simple patchwork in Scotland at the time of the Jacobite rising in 1745 but it does not seem to have been popular work—at least very little of it is known there nowadays. No trace of any cloth patchwork can be found which was made in England then, although it may have been made by the poorer people and has now perished.

A quilt of ivory silk, with a green and ivory *windmill* patchwork border, was discovered by Mrs Hake during her research into the quilting tradition of the south-western counties in 1934. The quilt was very worn and fragile and attempts to re-discover it have not been successful, but it was reliably dated as 1750.[1]

Loose covers of chintz were a fashionable protection for the valuable embroidered, velvet or damask upholstered chair-seats of the eighteenth century, and from about 1750 mention is made of them in patchwork and applied work also. Mrs Delaney described in her letters a set she made of linen, "in a most brilliant dark blue", bordered with a pattern of oak leaves cut out in white linen; she also made a coverlet to match. Other loose covers were made in patchwork and one of the earliest is illustrated on the kind of chair for which it was probably made during the second half of the century (*105*). The cover is one of a pair (possibly there was once a set) in *rosette* pattern and the materials show a variety of early wood-block prints, most of them dress linens and calicoes, with background patches of white twill and piqué. The colours of the typical small patterns are indigo, madder brown and black and lighter shades of rose, blue and neutral colours; some of the flower sprays, with the outlines drawn in black, have had the colour put in by "pencilling" (p. 29). The *dog's-tooth* border and the fringe are characteristic of many border patterns and finishes, until about 1830. Another remarkably pretty cover remains from what was also probably a set made about 1795; it is also in *rosette* pattern, with pink floral cotton patches set in a light brown ground of chintz.

No cotton patchwork of the mid-eighteenth century has yet been found but surviving quilts and coverlets made from 1780 onwards are comparatively numerous. In several of them, the patches have been cut from partly-worn embroideries and in others the embroidery has been worked on to the patches

[1] *English Quilting, Old and New*, E. Hake, Plate 12.

and designed to fit the outlines. A large coverlet already mentioned (p. 47) contains both these kinds of embroidery; the all-over *cotton-reel* pattern is not only arranged in opposite pairs of patches for their colour, but also with regard to the embroidered and printed French and Indian cottons. The patterns on both contain a variety of flower sprays (in *and* out of baskets and vases) and small figures of lizards, elephants, peacocks, lions and butterflies and many others. All the embroideries and prints are certainly earlier than 1790, when the work was done. A silk and velvet coverlet of the same date and similar design is in the Victoria and Albert Museum and illustrated in the Museum booklet.[1] Embroidery is also found as a border decoration in some patchwork and an example of this (also in the Museum) is illustrated on an unmounted cushion square, made in 1786 (*112*). A strip of calico, surrounding the centre *windmill* patchwork, is embroidered with a trailing leaf pattern in chain-stitch, and in spaces left for the purpose, the names HENRY – IANE – HAINES are worked in cross-stitch on three sides, while on the fourth is worked

SEPTEMBER THE 17 1786

HIH BORN

A noticeable crystallising of ideas and fashion in patchwork designs appears in those made in the last few years of the century. All-over mosaic patterns are

116　*Patchwork and appliqué flowers with striped ribbon*

drawn into orderly arrangements of groups and borders of different shapes and patterns. Applied work appears as an added decoration to geometrical patterns and, as will be seen, in the nineteenth-century work it takes the place of embroidery in most types of patchwork. Two pairs of bed hangings in *shell* pattern show a method of breaking up the all-over pattern into groups by means of outlining sections of the patches with green ribbon, after the work was completed (*113*). Another simple arrangement was making strips of patches in two different patterns, the length or width of the bed, which were joined together later. This idea was undoubtedly a forerunner of the traditional North Country striped or strip patterns. The illustrated coverlet (*111*) shows alternately patterned light and dark stripes made of geometrical patches, set in background patches of unbleached calico. It was made about 1780.

The design of the majority of coverlets, however, favoured a central panel,

---

[1] *Notes on Applied Work and Patchwork*, Plate 9.

framed by a series of borders. The centre, which was planned to lie on the top of the bed, just below the pillow (where it could be most admired), was more elaborately worked than the rest, but the borders gave great opportunity for a variety of different patterns in one piece of work. A coverlet made in Westmorland not later than 1795 shows a well-arranged pattern in a richly coloured collection of prints (*114*). The centre shows patchwork, with an appliqué floral pattern on borders of calico—the flowers are tied with striped *ribbon*. Three succeeding borders (or frames) of mosaic patterns—*double rosette*, *zig-zag* and three rows of *chained square*—in unfaded dark green, indigo and reddish purple are divided by strips of unbleached calico. The use of linen tape for the *zig-zag* pattern and the exact fitting of the pattern at the corners show unusually good planning. This work is also interesting, as its date was verified by numerous

117   *A Baby's Rattle*

118   *A Patchwork Duck*

manufacturers' marks and dated Excise stamps seen on the reverse side, several marked 1790 and 1792, and a calico strip has the name and date, "MARTHA JACKSON 1790", clearly written. The coverlet is unlined.

The fashion for having a padded day-time or top cover on the bed went out at about this time and, with a few exceptions, stayed out for thirty or forty years. Among these unpadded coverlets, a marriage coverlet of outstanding design and workmanship was made about 1790. It is illustrated (*104*) and described in some detail in Chapter Seven.

Except for the appliqué patterns, there is not much variety in the shapes which were used in most of the surviving quilts of the eighteenth century and it might be supposed from them that square, triangular, hexagonal and octagonal patches were all the shapes that had been evolved. That this is not so is proved beyond question by a coverlet in the Victoria and Albert Museum, dated 1797. It is as good as a pattern index or working sampler, in the number of mosaic and appliqué designs it contains. The work is built up of over two hundred squares in each of which is a pattern; there are between sixty and seventy different patterns. The applied patterns include flowers, birds, butterflies and a baby's rattle and a group of ducks have been so ingeniously pieced together from various coloured prints that a drawing is shown of the way in which one was made (*118*). Hemispheres in brown and white cotton, embroidered in yellow chain-stitch, occupy two of the outer corners, and opposite them maps of England and Scotland, with the counties marked by differently coloured cottons, fill the other two corners. An octagonal shape represents a sundial, with two hands indicating the figures "4" and "12"; below this is the date—1797—and, at a guess, it is possible that the numbers on the dial refer to a date also and may mean 4th December 1797 (*115*).

Many of the patterns in this coverlet do not appear in any other existing work of the century and some of them do not appear again for another fifty years or more, as far as can be told by patterns which have survived.

119 *Detail of fig. 120, showing polychrome cottons block-printed between 1800 and 1815*

120 *An unlined coverlet of large rectangular pieces surrounding a bordered centre panel showing a rural scene. c. 1815–20*

122 Part of the coverlet made by Jane, Cassandra and Mrs Austen, of polychrome block prints in a spotted white cotton ground. 1811

121 Detail of the valance in the Brereton bed hangings of block-printed cottons in coffin hexagons. c. 1801–04

124 *A marriage coverlet in cotton dress prints made by her mother for Sally Eaton, with her initials, hearts and kisses in hexagons. 1811*

123 *A coverlet in richly coloured cotton dress prints made by Elizabeth Jefferson, aged ten years. 1811*

125   *A coverlet in dark and richly-coloured dress and furnishing prints with a centre panel printed to commemorate the victory of the Duke of Wellington at the Battle of Vittoria. 1813*

CHAPTER TEN

THE NINETEENTH CENTURY

The manufacture of printed cotton increased with the coming of the nineteenth century and the fashion grew for using it in patchwork. Coverlets were "the thing" for the top covers and except for a certain number of cottage quilts (mostly from the North Country) very few interlined or padded quilts were made for this purpose until later in the century, although a number are found which are lightly quilted without an interlining. The designs were mostly of applied work, or with applied work patterns included as highlights of the general design; comparatively few coverlets were made entirely of patchwork until about 1830. The fashion for appliqué grew slowly, and at first quilts and coverlets which were made about the period dating from 1795 to 1805 had only a large central pattern containing some form of pictorial group with birds, flowers and trees—usually cut from the pattern of a length of printed cotton and applied to a background of geometrical patches. All the designs were planned to make the best use of the printed patterns: flowers were set in the centre of geometrical patches; striped materials were cut to make an orderly pattern when the patches were joined; and the geometrical patches were cut large enough to fit the printed designs.

Nineteenth-century coverlets were of immense size; some were a little smaller than those of the eighteenth century, but the beds were still of ample proportions and a set of furnishings in patchwork was a great undertaking. A large bed needed two large curtains, two yards in length and three and a half yards wide; two small curtains of the same length but one and a half yards wide; at least one valance on two sides and one end of the bed, six and a half yards long and twelve inches deep, and probably one or two rows of tester hangings of the same measurements. The headboards and tester ceilings were also upholstered—in several cases this was done in patchwork—and the crown of the work was, of course, the coverlet, which could measure anything from three to four yards square. A fully uphol-stered bed of patchwork, except for the coverlet, is shown in the Stranger's Hall, Norwich, and on the making of it hangs a true and romantic story. In 1782, Anna Margaretta Lloyd of Cardiganshire married her cousin, John Brereton, of Brinton Hall in Norfolk; their first baby died, but in 1786 a second boy arrived and he became the idol of his mother's heart. In April 1800, while at school, he fell ill with low fever from which he died, leaving his parents broken-hearted. For nearly a year his mother refused to be comforted but at length she was noticed to be designing patterns from pieces of material and joining them together. Gradually she became absorbed in her work and slowly forgot her sorrow in making the patchwork furnishings for her bed. By the time she had completed the work, she was entirely restored to health; a small part of the valance is illustrated (*121*) in which details of some contemporary chintz patterns (including a passion-flower print) are seen. Several of the *coffin* patches consist of small scraps joined to make the shape where the materials had been short.

Quite early in the nineteenth century we find quilts and coverlets known to have been made by children. By the end of the eighteenth century samplers worked in cross-stitch, with their pathetic and pious little verses and texts, had come to be considered as a conventional part of every girl's education in the schools as well as at home. They were also taught the essentials of "plain" sewing and patchwork was (and still is) a good exercise in the necessary routine stitches of running, seaming and hemming, while learning also the proper way of handling materials and how to manage needle and thread. Great concentration was undoubtedly needed to complete a sampler, but the dogged diligence and enterprise called for in an attempt at making a patchwork quilt at the tender age of eight or nine years showed great strength of purpose. Elizabeth Jefferson was ten when she made her coverlet of richly coloured dress prints and a great variety of patterns in patchwork and appliqué (*123*). She embroidered her name, age and the date on a small square in the centre:

ELIZABETH JEFFERSON

AGED 10 YEARS

1811

and her purpose for the future showed no less enterprise, as she clearly intended this as her marriage coverlet and included *hearts* among the patterns. Another achievement on the same scale, but about thirty years later, was that of Jennet Maudesley, who lived in a gaunt old Yorkshire farmhouse—the only girl in a family of eight children. By the time she was eleven she had completed a patchwork coverlet measuring ten feet square; three years later, in 1846, she died at the age of fourteen (six months after her mother), and her father took the coverlet which she had used on her bed—signed and dated JENNET MAUDESLEY, 1843—and folded it away in memory of his daughter.

Smaller things such as cushion covers and pincushions were made by children and some velvet antimacassars in *diamond* patches ("made from ball-gowns of the landed gentry"), which did not wear out for over a hundred years, were the work of a girl of ten, apprenticed to a dressmaker in 1837. Her father was the village blacksmith and she had seven brothers and two sisters and a mother of Huguenot descent, who was "small, vivacious and most thrifty, never wasting a pin"— which virtues were inherited by her daughter. Much patchwork was done in the dames' schools; simple *rosette* patterns or the *windmill* or *cotton-reel* seem to have been the most popular. An unfinished coverlet, begun about 1840 in a Yorkshire village school is typical of many made throughout the century. A centre of *honeycomb* patches is clearly the work of the teacher; the surrounding *rosettes* of coloured dress prints in a calico ground are sewn with long stitches, short stitches, clean white stitches and "shady" white ones; some are small and even and some look like a row of broken palings, producing a strong conviction that the small boys had been included in the sewing class.

Many women can still remember that as children they were not allowed out to play until they had made their daily number of patches, ready to be sewn into the quilt in the evening. *Rosettes* contained a convenient number of patches for this—for the younger children at least and the older ones were expected to do more. This daily work was generally put into a family effort but many individual coverlets were made only for best occasions (the marriage coverlets for the very best) and nearly all of them were kept as heirlooms and handed down to the eldest daughter or son. Sometimes they were bequeathed to the member of the family in each generation bearing the same Christian name as the maker—to the Marys, Elizabeths, or Alices and so on—of a family. A number of the coverlets illustrated are heirlooms; some of them, as the Levens Hall quilt (*110*), have never left the house in which they were made, others have been across the world and back— two of them (*114, 127*) to Australia and New Zealand and nearly all those which are not in museums have been inherited by descendants of the makers. Arabella Gwatkin's coverlet has been handed down for six generations; Jane Austen's still belongs to one of her descendants. A Yorkshire heirloom has a letter which goes with it, written on 12th November 1908; it reads:

> Dear Faith,
>
> I wanted dear G. Parents things kept in the family. . . . G. Mother's quilt to pass to Eva when you have done with it. Tell her our G. Mother patched it before she was married. She was 26 when she married, a wife over 50 years and she has been in heaven 46 years, so it must be nearly if not quite 100 years old and there is no patchwork like it nowadays. Some of the octagons are in 3 pieces to form the pattern, one is done wrong way round. It was a young man's planning and the linen is very fine. I know you will value it. . . .
>
> Your affectionate cousin,
> Maggie Headlands.

The "octagons" are, in fact, hexagons and the quilt now belongs to Faith's great-niece. The "young man's planning" is a design with an appliqué centre of the floral patterns typical of the early 1800s, surrounded with hexagon borders and finished with a *dog's-tooth* edge.

The diamond-patterned quilt made by Mrs Austen and her gifted daughters, Jane and Cassandra, is recorded in a letter written by Jane to her sister (away on a visit), saying, "Have you collected the pieces for the patchwork? We are at a standstill". It was written in 1811, the year in which *Sense and Sensibility* was published, and the coverlet is now kept at the Austens' house in Chawton, Hampshire.

The commemorative block-printed panels which were fashionable at the beginning of the century are illustrated. One has already been described (p. 30), and was used in quilts made about King George III's jubilee year, 1810, and the other (*125*), to celebrate the victory of Wellington at Vittoria, is printed in much the same colours, with an arc of yellow and red flame over Wellington's name. Other victories and occasions of the time do not seem to have been immortalised in patchwork patterns, except for pieces of the "Nelson" print used in the coverlet begun after the Battle of the Nile (p. 31) and the octagonal panel printed on the occasion of Princess Charlotte's marriage to Prince Leopold (p. 31). Plate-printed pictorial patterns on cotton and linen had been popular from time to time since the eighteenth century and scenes of the death and funeral of Lord Nelson were among the contemporary prints, but though they had a topical interest they did not inspire the quilt-makers of the day. Admiral Collingwood seems to have been the last of the famous people so honoured in patchwork at that time.

The specially printed panels used in the early nineteenth-century "framed" designs appear to be the immediate forerunners of the all-appliqué coverlets which were to become so widely popular towards the end of the Georgian period. The Jefferson (*123*) and Eaton (*124*) coverlets show two kinds of framed pattern, one partly appliqué, one all-geometrical, and both made about the same year. The two commemorative quilts just mentioned are typical of another stage. Arabella Gwatkin combines cut-out chintz appliqué with borders of geometrical shapes in 1816 (*130*), also Mary Dickinson, in 1815, did appliqué in natural leaf and flower shapes and combined it with geometrical patchwork (*132*). Each worker uses the Portuguese hem to produce the *dog's-tooth* borders and not separate triangular patches, but the Dickinson coverlet having *hearts* among the patterns is a marriage coverlet and is signed and dated and has also the name of the Durham village where it was made:

MARY

DICKINSON

THORNLEY

1815

Patchwork was one of the occupations taught to the women in Newgate

126　*A marriage coverlet in patchwork with appliqué patterns of hearts and natural leaf and flower shapes, in colours of light blue, pink, tan and buff with dark blue and green cotton dress prints. Made by Mary Dickinson of Thornley. Dated 1815*

127 *A Durham flower-basket quilt with baskets of pale shaded green cotton and flowers and leaves of red and green calico. c. 1830*

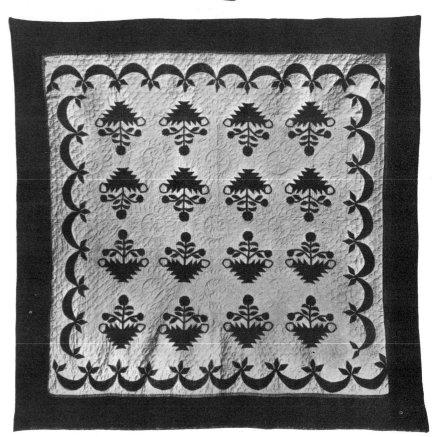

128 *A flower-basket quilt in Devonshire with red baskets and flowers and leaves in red and green cotton. The hammock border is dark green. Early nineteenth century*

129 *The centre of an appliqué coverlet in red, pink and blue cotton prints, herringbone-stitched to a calico backing. c. 1815*

130 *A chintz coverlet in brown and pink chintz appliqué with many coloured patchwork borders, made by Arabella Gwatkin. c. 1812*

131   *The "Isle of Wight" coverlet with appliqué and patchwork patterns in chintz and
cotton dress prints. c. 1820*

Prison by Elizabeth Fry, who realised the good effect of giving them cheerful community work to do. In her life of Mrs Fry, Mrs Janet Whitney describes how a member of the Society of Friends sat at the head of a long table reading aloud to the women who did their work, each wearing a clean blue apron and bib, with a numbered ticket on a red tape hanging round her neck. Even those who were sentenced to transportation for life were provided with all the patchwork materials they would need on the long voyage to New South Wales, as patchwork

132   *Borders in Mary Dickinson's coverlet with hearts and natural leaves of oak,*
ash and ivy

had a ready sale there. Some of the work was disposed of on the way and in 1819 one of the ships touched at Rio de Janeiro where quilts were sold for one guinea each. Recent attempts to trace any quilts sold in New South Wales have been unsuccessful so far and only two coverlets are known at present to be associated with the work of Elizabeth Fry; both have been bequeathed to the Castle Museum at Norwich.

It is possible that at no other period was patchwork so universally made in England as during the years from 1800 until the beginning of Queen Victoria's reign. Appliqué is more typical than other kinds of patchwork and the number of coverlets which have been preserved in mint condition speaks for the value which was put upon them. Never again do we find work which compares with them for colour or pattern. Isolated pieces of good work appear before this time, such as the eighteenth-century coverlet mentioned in Chapter IX (p. 103) and another but of a different kind made about 1815, the centre of which is illustrated. The "Isle of Wight" coverlet (*131*), presumably made about 1820, is yet another in which some flower patterns are made of geometrical patterns (*133, 134*) and it is probable that a laurel leaf was used as a template for the garland and sprays. The Sharman sisters designed their appliqué from their own garden flowers about the same time and their patterns are finely hemmed to a ground of unbleached calico (*116*). Two very similar coverlets were made (probably as a pair) about 1820, each

133 A horn-of-plenty with patchwork flowers, in the Isle of Wight quilt

134 Spray of flowers in the Isle of Wight quilt

with the familiar "Pheasant and Palm" design in the centre and in the one illustrated (*144*) four peacocks and four peahens keep him company. Among roses, passion-flowers, tulips, daisies, poppies and other flower patterns nine different kinds of birds fly or perch. The colours are still brilliant; bright blues, strong greens and reds predominate and the flowers, printed in natural colours, are hemmed to a ground of unbleached calico. A bolder design was used in the coverlet made about 1825 (*140*) and the flower patterns are set off by the use of dark prints in a pattern of twisted ribbon and a *dog's-tooth* border, all hemmed to a ground of thick white cotton. An appliqué coverlet made in Newark about 1825 has loops and festoons of linked hexagons and diamonds (*135*) with patchwork flower patterns (*136*) scattered among pieces cut from eighteenth-century embroideries.

The appliqué patterns mentioned so far have been of the manor-house rather than the cottage, but the simpler patterns made by village people are no less interesting. The two *flower-basket* quilts (*127, 128*) which show a different outlook on the same pattern and the appliqué version of the *pincushion* found in North

135 *Looped festoons of hexagon and diamond patches in applied work*

Country quilts are typical of true village work. Patterns made by cottage workers are generally of a more constant and steadfast tradition than the upper-class work

136 *Patchwork flower patterns made from diamonds*

and less influenced by changes in fashion. They have used patchwork patterns of many kinds and adapted them to appliqué, probably because dress prints were more available than the flowered chintzes and not all had the skill and imagination needed, even for patterns such as Mary Dickinson's or the anonymous master-piece mentioned in Chapter VII (p. 82).

Flowered cotton prints can be found in quilts made during the twenty or thirty years following the end of the Georgian period, but a gradual change in

137   *Other patchwork flower patterns*

the designs shows less and less applied work and an increase in the use of smaller patterned cottons. Silk and velvet pieces in geometrical patterns by slow degrees replaced the chintz appliqué of the manor-house, as the dress fashion for these materials also changed. About the 1830s muslin appeared in some coverlets, but examples of it now are rare; the illustrated *brick* pattern (*146*) is made from mauve,

138   *An appliqué version of the pincushion*

blue, purple and brown muslins with printed and woven designs; the coverlet is still in use but nothing is known of its history except that it appeared in a jumble sale and was rescued from there. An example of a fashion which lasted from the eighteenth century until the early 1900s is a small pocket (one of a pair) made in the *cotton-reel* pattern about 1835 (*153*). These pockets were worn in pairs connected with tape and tied around the waist, above the petticoat and under a full-skirted dress; they were reached by slits in the side seams. The cushion square made by Miss Lucy Brett of Norfolk (*141*) during the 1830s is a good example of the contemporary patterns, with its clear outline enclosing a number of colours. Miss Brett was well-known for her needlework and not only made the coverlet in the same *star* pattern (p. 59) but she is also remembered for winning a bet that she would make a "gentleman's shirt" complete with frills in one day, providing she was allowed to cut it out the day before. The *diamond* pattern on another coverlet of the time also encloses a combination of colours (*147*);

139 *An appliqué coverlet in finely-cut natural flower patterns and some patchwork in the centre. Delicate colours on a calico ground with an outer border of a print added later. A small piece of the original border can be seen. Made by two Miss Sharmans. c. 1820*

140 *An appliqué coverlet with floral chintz patterns in russet brown and yellow. The centre medallion and dog's-tooth border are dark green cotton with red polka dots. Date said to be 1825*

141 *A cushion square with star pattern in pink and dark green hexagons as made by Lucy Brett. c. 1836*

142 *A cot cover of red and white gathered hexagons with red diamonds and pyramids, made by Isabella Cruddas in Rookhope. c. 1850*

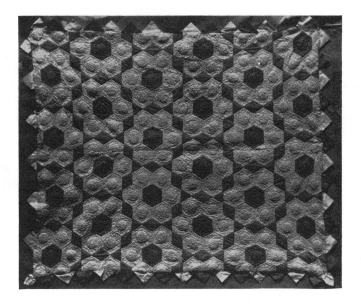

143 *An appliqué and patchwork quilt in bright richly-coloured cottons. The appliqué bows are blue and the quilting follows the patchwork pattern. Made by Mary Loyd in Cardiganshire. 1840*

144 *One of two cotton appliqué coverlets which are almost alike. The birds and flowers are in bright strong natural colours. c. 1820*

145   *An appliqué coverlet with a great variety of patterns in cotton prints on a calico ground. It was probably intended as a marriage coverlet. c. 1850. The two female figures in the centre were clearly copied from Hiram Power's celebrated "Greek Slave" statue shown in the Great Exhibition of 1851*

146 *A coverlet made of late Georgian muslins in pale blue, lavender, purple and brown colours. c. 1830*

147 *A diamond-patterned coverlet in hexagons of red, russet, brown and yellow chintz in a calico ground. c. 1835*

it will be seen that some of the groups are cut from one piece of chintz, carefully shaped at the edges so that they appear to be made of separate pieces.

The affection for floral applied work took some time to die but quilts made about 1840 retain only shadows of the earlier patterns. Small appliqué cornucopias and a basket of flowers appear among the *rosette* patterns on a coverlet made in this year, which was shown eleven years later at the Great Exhibition (*150*). With the exception of these patterns in a dark blue print, the cottons are all mauve, blue and pink dress prints, typical of those used until the end of the century; the work is finished with a frill of pink and white striped cotton, which was the fashionable finish and took the place of the fringe on the edge of quilts until the early years of the next century. Mary Loyd's quilt (signed and dated 1840) is more like the earlier applied work (*143*); it has one of the "bird and tree" patterns surrounded by an appliqué leaf garland (*67*) in dark green on a calico ground. The cut-out chintz patterns in the corners of the centre square are in many bright colours and bows of bright blue cotton add to the pattern of this Cardiganshire quilt—one of the best of its period. It is interlined with wool and the quilting is in *diamond* pattern, except where it follows the appliqué in the centre.

An unorthodox kind of *honeycomb* pattern first seems to have been done at this time. Each patch consists of two hexagonal pieces of cotton (no silk work has ever been found), one of which is a little larger than the other; the larger piece is gathered at the sides to make each equal to the length of those on the smaller hexagon; they were then joined, one above the other, so that together they made one patch. The fullness in the middle of the upper layer was gathered in also, and sewn down to the lower patch, thus giving the effect of a small rosette. After washing and ironing the gathers tended to flatten and give a depressing appearance to this kind of work, but in a cot quilt made by Isabella Cruddas of Rookhope, County Durham, a small amount of padding was gathered into the centre of each hexagon, which held the fullness and preserved the rosette effect. The little quilt illustrated is in red and white calico hexagons, outlined with a pattern of *diamonds* and *pyramids* of red calico. It is lined with calico and finished with a border of alternate red and white pyramids (*142*).

From time to time men have taken an interest in patchwork and there is no doubt that the earliest known example was made by them (p. 21). Men designed and made patchwork in this country from the beginning of the nineteenth century and from about 1840 there is constant evidence that fathers and sons made a considerable contribution to the work of the family; not only did they cut the templates but also the papers and materials and often helped with the sewing. A Somerset woman can remember "helping Father to get on with the patchwork when Mother got tired of it"; a "young man's planning" (p. 111) resulted in an outstanding pattern of applied and patchwork; in 1837 Elizabeth Cakebread's father (he was a parson) designed a quilt for her in hexagons, which she never finished.[1] Joe the Quilter, the Northumbrian character famous for his quilting designs, made patchwork tops for his quilts. Quite a number of them have survived, especially around Hedley, where he lived before his mysterious murder in 1825, and one is illustrated in *Traditional Quilting*. Several contain pieces of the "pheasant and palm-tree" print.

In 1854 Private Thomas Walker was wounded in the head at the battle of Inkerman; his skull was repaired by a silver plate, and to add to this interesting attraction of Private Walker, he spent his time of convalescence sitting up in bed making a patchwork coverlet and was seen in Fort Pitt military hospital by Queen Victoria while on an official visit in March 1855. The illustration (*152*) is taken from a painting by Thomas Wood (1856) which now hangs in the Royal College of Surgeons at Lincoln's Inn Fields and is an interesting reminder that the value of what is now known as Occupational Therapy was recognised over a hundred years ago. During the war from 1939 until 1945, patchwork was included in the occupational parcels of different kinds of handwork sent to British prisoners of war in overseas prison camps. A beautifully made work-bag is cherished by the family of a man who was confined to an invalid's chair for many years; he not only did patchwork but made a work-drawer to fit under his chair, so that his work was always on hand. Sailors are well-known for their nimble fingers and several are known to have done patchwork. A long and narrow coverlet made to fit a ship's bunk was worked by a "sailor of Bristol city" about ninety years ago in black and red cloth *diamonds*, embroidered with flags and ensigns; a Durham monumental sculptor made himself a silk smoking-cap, during his off-duty hours while working his passage to America in 1866—it also is embroidered with naval emblems and contains brocade pieces from furnishings in the Duke of Marlborough's house, given to him by a lady's maid there. The work of James Williams (*156*) and Mr Walter White (*175*) is illustrated.

Crazy work was popular in the 1880s; we read that "only those having seen this fashionable work can imagine its beauty for pillows and quilts . . . it is not only confined to quilts and cushions—very handsome piano-covers, antimacassars, sofa-pillows, table-covers, etc. can be arranged"; many of these furnishings were made "en suite" for the parlour. Cushions and coverlets in *box* pattern were universally admired and loose covers for chair-seats were often made of it. Beds were still furnished entirely in patchwork and two sets (one for "best") were made for a Dorset half-tester bed about 1870 and many of the *diamonds* contain the embroidered initials of the makers.

[1] *Notes on Applied Work and Patchwork*, plate 10.

An unusual piece of patchwork seems rightly to belong to the second half of the nineteenth century, although if the story attached to it could be proven it would add another one and a half centuries to the history of English patchwork. It is a silk chasuble, reputed to have been made during the time of the Reformation and carried in his pack together with small sacramental vessels, by a priest disguised as a pedlar. The illustration shows the pattern on the back of the vestment, with the main pattern made from rows of four-point *stars* in black silk, joined by light-coloured *diamonds* as illustrated in a border pattern of the 1880s. Several other patterns in the design are cruciform in arrangement (*155*, *148*). The colours of the silks compare closely with a similar pattern of a cushion cover in clear pink and yellow with black, made about 1860 (*154*).

A great deal of work in silk, satin, silk and velvet, or a mixture of all three, often supplemented by pieces of woollen cloth and cotton, was made during the

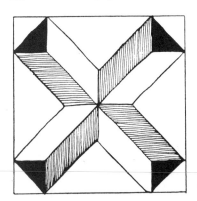 

148 *Patterns with three-dimensional effect made of rhomboids and triangles in the chasuble*

last forty years of the century. No account could have been given to the wearing quality of such work, with the result that most of it is more ragged and worn than cotton coverlets of twice its age. *Box* pattern was made mostly of silk, or silk and velvet; *crazy* work and *log-cabin* were of silk and velvet or of any available pieces of all kinds of material put together; many of these have now disappeared. Quilts in good-quality silks and velvets, however, have lasted well. Three of them have been mentioned (p. 32) and also a reference made (p. 68) to Jenny Jones' *crazy* coverlet (*163*), which is surely one of the best of its kind. The silk, satin and velvet pieces are of the first quality, most in darkish shades of all colours; the embroidery contains much *ribbon work* in flower sprays and figures of children, birds and flowers are worked in embroidery stitches. The outer border consists of a dark moss-green velvet, worked with running sprays of roses and forget-me-nots in fine ribbon work. An illustrated log-cabin bed-cover is made entirely of velvet in scarlet, purple, crimson, blue, gold, bright yellow, and green; two other log-cabin coverlets were acquired by chance—one bought in the Caledonian Market (*166*) is a mixture of silk, tweed, flannel velvet and so on and the other (*157*)—bought for two shillings at a jumble sale in Deptford—has centre squares of red plush, "logs" of good satins, and is lined with cotton Paisley. The North Country strip quilts illustrated were made towards the end of the century and also the appliqué marriage quilt (*162*) with the quilting *feather* in the centre.

The last forty years were remarkable for the number of small things, other than quilts, which were made. Loose covers for chair-seats were still fashionable and they appear also for piano stools in the 1870s; patchwork for hand-screens,

149　*Pincushions to be suspended by a ribbon from a nail in the wall*

firescreens, glove and handkerchief sachets, blinds and "window-sill valances", finished with fringed and scalloped edges, were recommended. A tea-cosy and matching kettle-holder were a social asset, also egg-cosies; one made of *crazy work* and large enough to cover a goose-egg is lavishly embroidered and, to prevent any attempt to put it on the tea-pot, "EGG 1891" has been added in stem-stitch. Fashion notes included muffs made of velvet; Weldon's *Practical Publications* suggested that "an elegant bag for holding work is always a desirable acquisition and if it be handsome enough to take occasionally to the theatre to contain handkerchief, opera glasses and smelling bottle so much the better".

Pincushions were often fitted into the small compartments of work-box trays (two in a matching pattern, used separately for pins and needles) made of *box* or

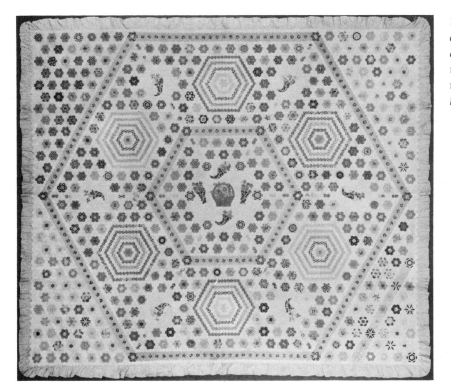

150 *A coverlet of cotton dress prints in rosettes and hexagon patterns, with some appliqué. It was shown in 1851 at the Great Exhibition. 1840*

151 *A silk coverlet notable for its adapted quilting pattern of the running feather, carried out in green and black silks. Other patterns have strong connections with quilting. The reverse side is of patchwork also. Nineteenth century*

153 *A patchwork pocket worn under the skirt. c. 1835*

152 *A painting by T. W. Wood of Private Thomas Walker making a cloth coverlet in Fort Pitt Military Hospital. 1856*

155 *Silk chasuble. Date unknown*

154 *Cushion cover made from black, pink and yellow satin ribbons. c. 1860*

156 *A coverlet of inlaid felt pieces with biblical pictures and scenes of the engineering wonders of Wales made in ten years by James Williams of Wrexham. 1842–52*

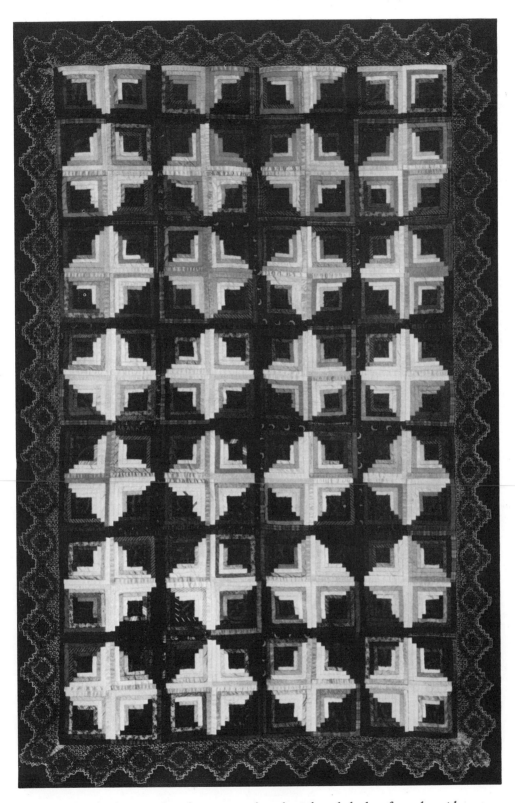

157　*A Log-cabin coverlet of satins, mostly red, pink and shades of purple, with centre squares of crimson plush and edged with string lace. c. 1860*

158 *An unmounted silk chair-seat cover of blue, lilac, cream and white "boxes" set in a black ground. Made by Mrs Durie of Pensford, Somerset. 1870*

159 *A Northumbrian pincushion quilt of Turkey red and white calico. The same pattern is called "Peter and Paul" in Somerset. c. 1870*

160 *Detail of a Durham quilt showing the quilting following the patchwork. c. 1890*

161 *A Devonshire quilt with a centre pattern of square and octagonal pieces. c. 1870*

162   *A Northumberland quilt with appliqué version of the quilting feather pattern in red and green calico on a white ground. c. 1870–75*

163　*A crazy-work coverlet of embroidered silk, brocade and velvet made by Jenny Jones. 1884*

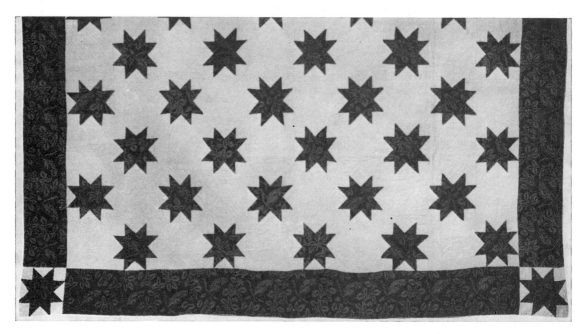

164 *Part of a Red Star block quilt of red cotton and white calico made in County Durham. c. 1890*

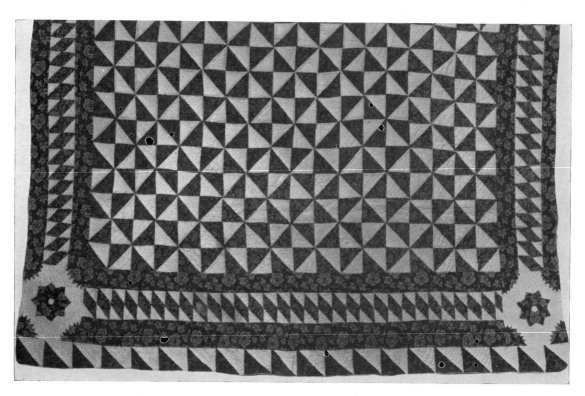

165 *Part of a Windmill quilt made in County Durham of rose-patterned red cotton and white calico. c. 1890*

166   *Part of a Log-cabin couvre-pieds of tweed, silk, flannel and velvet.*
Late nineteenth century

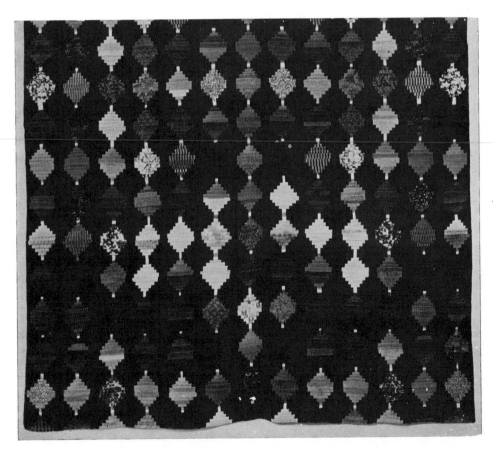

167   *Part of a velvet Log-cabin bed cover in scarlet, purple, pink, crimson, blue,*
yellow, green and gold. c. 1880

168 *A patchwork picture now in the Shakespeare Memorial Theatre at Stratford-on-Avon, of a Christmas christening in the parish church at Stratford, made by Mrs H. R. Harris. 1876*

star patterns and other covers and linings were also made of patchwork. Pincushions were looked upon as "pretty ornaments for the drawing-room table or suspended from a nail in the wall". Three hanging pincushions shown are taken from Weldon's of 1885. A collection of pincushions at Gawthorpe Hall (now National Trust property) near Burnley include a variety of shapes, includ-

169 *A bead-embroidered star in green and white*

170 *A jug in white-beaded plum-colour and blue-beaded white quarterings*

ing one in a *box and star* shape (*169*), two resembling small jugs with pins in the "lids" (*170, 171*), one as a jockey cap (*172*), and many others, including a *pentagon* ball.

Any story of the century's work would be incomplete without mention of the patchwork pictures made by an old lady of Stratford-upon-Avon, Mrs H. R.

171 *A jug in white-beaded red and blue-beaded white quarterings*

172 *A jockey cap with black peak and quarterings of pink and green*

Harris, which are now in the Shakespeare Memorial Theatre. She lived in a very small cottage not far from the Shakespeare Hotel and the walls of her room were hung with her pictures, which she delighted to show to visitors and charged a penny "to see the exhibition". One of her visitors can remember her in 1912 at seventy years old, as "a very spry little woman with bright black eyes". The picture illustrated (*168*) is of a Christmas christening service—perhaps in 1875 as it is signed and dated H. R. HARRIS 1876. The figures gathered round the font have skirts, coats, hats and trousers made from actual pieces of tweed, suiting, velvet and cloth (except for the lady in a striped skirt made of pillow ticking), and the baby's long gown is a piece of broderie anglaise. The Christmas "decorations" are worked in green wool. Many other pictures made by this old lady are in the theatre, no less interesting than the christening.

CHAPTER ELEVEN

THE TWENTIETH CENTURY

The turn of the century saw no great change in the kind of patchwork from that which had been made for the last forty years, but it is clear to see, on looking back, that its popularity had fallen. Social conditions were changing and women's interests were taking on a greater freedom, from the entirely domestic round to out-of-door occupations such as walking, bicycling and tennis playing. Many more people were able to read and daily papers brought the up-to-date doings of the world in general into the country districts. Needlework encyclopedias and instruction books on "fancy work" turned their readers' enthusiasms to crochet work, macramé, "open work" and tatting; quilting and patchwork were not even mentioned—they were old-fashioned and out.

The momentum of the nineteenth-century enthusiasm carried the work along for the first ten years of the twentieth century, but by the beginning of the "Kaiser's War" there seems to have been comparatively little patchwork done except by the older women. Materials were cheap and plentiful; quilts could be made from whole lengths and there was not the necessity for patchwork, except where habitual thrift was too strong and the work was done almost automatically whenever there were pieces to be used up. Workers in the North Country were steadfast in the tradition of the simple two-colour patterns made in plain calicoes and cottons, such as the red printed cotton and white calico *windmill* (165) and *red star* (164) quilts from Ireshopeburn and Rookhope in County Durham, a *feathered star* (178) in pink zephyr gingham from Allendale Town in Northumberland, and another Durham quilt with applied patchwork *baskets* of red and white calico from St John's Chapel (177). In other parts of the country *crazy work* and *box* pattern of taffeta and velvet and pieces of the "new" artificial silk were made. Along with many undistinguished patterns, honeycomb quilts consisting of a mass of multicoloured pieces were put together with no planned pattern; even the simple *rosette* pattern was often obscured by thick striped shirtings and Turkey twill centre pieces, joined without the relief of a background in unbleached calico. A few *rosette* coverlets made of small spot-patterned, striped and check dress prints in blue, pink and mauve have survived and are still fresh and pretty, but most of the work was roughly made, with monotonous sameness in its lack of pattern and colour. Scalloped frills were a fashionable finish to many patterns, especially in South Wales.

One coverlet (still unlined) was begun by Mr Walter White of Bepton in Sussex in the early years of this century (175). The blue satin pieces of his mother's wedding dress are matched with other blue pieces in cotton and set off by *baskets*, *stars* and hexagonal and triangular arrangements in various reds and flowered white prints; each patch is little more than one-quarter of an inch across; put in with meticulous care and small neat stitches. Mr White still enjoys recalling how he did his patchwork while he was on duty as a night-watchman on road work—"sitting in my cabin"—while guarding the newly-acquired steam roller belonging to the Midhurst District Council.

In spite of a general decline of interest in patchwork, it never ceased altogether to be made wherever there was a need for a cheap bedcover. Forty or fifty years ago comparatively few of the young women took up the work which they would have been expected to do as a daily task some fifty years earlier, with the result that to many of the women who do it nowadays the tradition was handed on by their grandmothers—not by their mothers. There is a lost generation of patchwork-makers from the beginning of the war in 1914 until well into the 1920s.

In 1928 Mrs FitzRandolph discovered, in the course of her work, a number of old patchwork quilts treasured for their patterns, but little contemporary work being done in places where a characteristic tradition had been maintained for over one and a half centuries.

It became clear by the early 1930s that the making of patchwork was increasing in other country districts in England, wherever members of a village or hamlet could work together. Individual workers were comparatively few, and even the old idea of the "family" quilt had been forgotten, but working parties of about twelve women who met once a week to make a coverlet under the leadership of one of their number (shades of Newgate Prison!) became an occasion in village life in the winter months. The possibility of raising money by raffling or selling patchwork was usually the reason behind the work and a number of charities and other good causes (such as the "boiler fund" for church or chapel or a new lighting system for the village hall) were supported in this way. A good example of a simple pattern was made by a working party in the small Somerset village of Allerton in 1935, when the quilt they made was raffled for the church funds. The centre pattern consisted of six diamond-shaped groups of hexagons. Each group was filled with brightly-coloured cotton patches and outlined with a single row of black, brown or darkish grey; the groups were then arranged to make a star pattern set in a white ground for the centre of the work, with smaller stars in the four corners. The coverlet was finished with a border of single diamond groups. Five pounds was considered a handsome sum to raise in the days when raffle tickets were sold for twopence or threepence each.

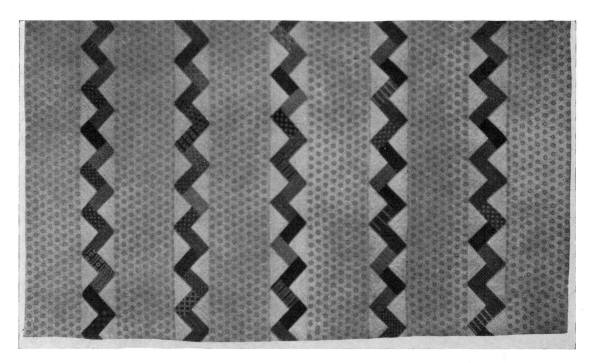

173　*Part of a zig-zag strip quilt of purple and creamy-buff printed cottons. Late nineteenth century*

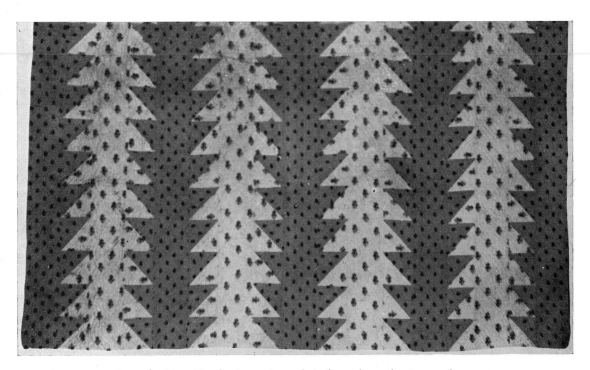

174　*Part of a Tree Everlasting strip quilt in lavender and primrose dress cottons.*
Late nineteenth century

175 *A coverlet of over seventeen thousand pieces in red, white and blue made by Mr Walter White of Bepton in Sussex. c. 1920*

176 *A Pineapple quilt in red and white calico made in Westmorland by Miss Annie Thompson of Natland. 1920*

177 *A white calico block quilt with forty-two appliqué patchwork baskets in red calico. 1910*

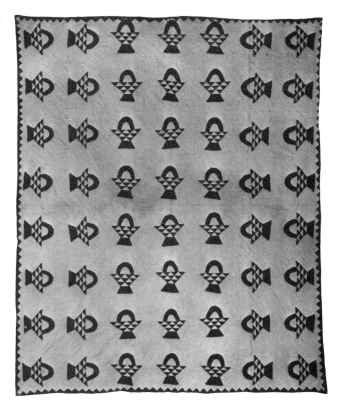

178 *A Feathered Star block quilt in pink zephyr gingham and white calico made in Allendale Town, Northumberland. 1910*

179　*The Brick Wall pattern in a Durham quilt of red "bricks" and calico "cement". c. 1890*

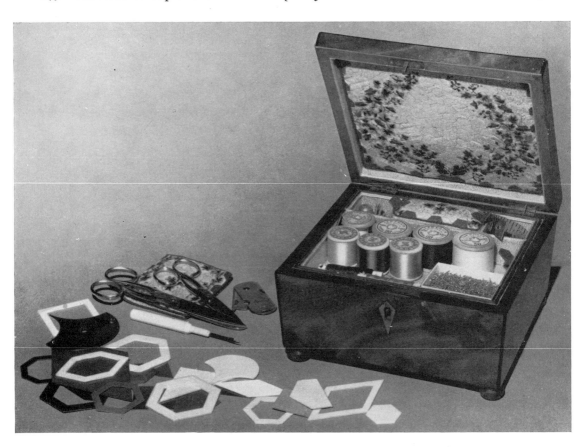

180　*A work-box with the usual contents as well as seam-ripper, razor blade in a holder and a collection of templates needed for patchwork. Patchwork fittings in the box, designed and made by Averil Colby*

Amateur dramatic societies found patchwork an economical and appropriate way of making stage curtains for village halls, and in North Somerset they are a feature of the stage furnishings in the villages of Backwell, Congresbury, Monkton Combe and Claverton Down. The village hall at Ellingham in the New Forest also possesses patchwork stage curtains and possibly there are others, as yet undiscovered.

Examples of patchwork usually have been included in exhibitions run by arts and crafts societies and other organisations interested in traditional crafts; the exhibits are often old pieces of work, but many of them also are newly made. Exhibitions of country crafts in London organised by the National Federation of Women's Institutes, in 1932, 1935 and 1938, included good pieces of work among the quilts and coverlets as well as smaller articles such as curtains, cushion-covers, tea-cosies and pincushions, which always have been included in the patchwork repertoire. Miss Alice Armes, who was a Durham woman and had been brought up in surroundings of patchwork and quilting, did a great deal to stimulate and encourage the making of patchwork among the country women with whom she worked while she was Handicrafts Organiser for the Women's Institutes. Renewed interest brought a demand for instruction in making patchwork, which out-ran the supply of mother-to-daughter method of teaching and, towards the end of the 1930s, it was a recognised subject for classes of adults in the villages. The "teaching" was often given by women whose only qualification was that they "had picked it up" from someone else and were prepared to hand on their knowledge, but much good work was done by them. These amateur teachers had a great deal of encouragement and help from Miss Muriel Rose, whose knowledge and experience has done so much towards keeping alive the best in traditional work; her interest in patchwork is largely responsible for the life and vigour of the present-day work. Quilts made at Much Hadham in which Miss Rose had a personal interest (p. 35) were shown at exhibitions in London and their style and patterns set a standard for a great deal of the work which has been done since in simple arrangements of colour and the appreciation of white as a background. It says much for the work which was done immediately before "Hitler's War" that it survived the disruption of the country's way of life. It was a very popular kind of work once more and with the coming of the war the enthusiasm for it was turned to making bedcovers for use in hospitals, convalescent homes for civilians or soldiers, and hostels run for men and women on leave from the services.

The quality of the patterns fell from grace again and there was, from necessity, little discrimination about the kind of materials which were used; everything was "grist" and into the patchwork it went. The coverlets were made also to meet the inevitable necessity for raising money by raffles and sales. Girl Guides in Lancashire "sold" *diamond* patches—"sixpence each or four for two shillings"—for a quilt they made in aid of a service charity and afterwards presented it to Waddon Hall (the Girl Guide Training Centre at Clitheroe) as an example of English traditional work. Men and women on "fire-watching" duty in more than one air-raid warden's post passed the time on quiet nights in doing patchwork. One of them was made as a *signature* quilt and the pencilled signatures of the wardens were embroidered over in simple stitchery.[1] Civilians on unaccustomed and difficult jobs made patchwork in their spare moments for relaxation. A war-time driver "made a lot of patchwork during the war, as I found it a soothing restorative when I came in from driving miles in the black-out". The unwarlike centre of the coverlet in Figure *181* is unforgettably associated with the arrival of Hitler's second-in-command, Rudolf Hess, in Scotland in 1941; it was completed on that day. A number of village communities in the south-west made patchwork coverlets for St Loye's Training College for disabled persons in Exeter, and beds at the headquarters of the Red Cross Society in London are furnished with patchwork covers, as are many other establishments connected with voluntary and charitable organisations. Patterns in applied patchwork also enlivened the hems and borders of black-out curtains made necessary by war-time conditions.

The end of the war in 1945 did not bring the end of textile rationing, which was to last for another six years, and so there was still a genuine need for economy. Many women who had been drawn into work-parties during the war, in which they had learned to do patchwork, began to make it for themselves, not only for the sake of the economy, but for the satisfaction they found in the colour and pattern-making. A great number of the work-parties did not disband, but continued to meet and do patchwork during the winter months each year, held together by their pleasure in the work and the mutual interest and companionship. With the shortage of materials and clothing, it was only natural that some attempts were made to make some kinds of garments of patchwork; not all were successful. Waistcoats made from tailors' cloth patterns were adequate and warm; dressing-gowns and jackets filled a need and left the rationed materials to be made into more essential daytime garments. Short capes, shawls (made from soft woollen pieces), collars, cuffs and belts helped to keep the wardrobes going and some enterprising workers made indoor and bedroom slippers with uppers of patchwork. Ecclesiastical vestments—three of them are copes—have been made in recent years. One in *honeycomb* hexagons was made by parishioners for the new church of St Christopher's in Southbourne, Hampshire. Another, completed

[1] *Patchwork*, Margaret Agutter.

in the spring of 1957, is made throughout of two-inch *diamond* patches and three crosses are incorporated in the design—one on the back of the work and one below each shoulder. The third cope (*185*) was the work of women in the Cotswold village of Burford and was given to the parish church in commemoration of the coronation of Queen Elizabeth the Second. The pieces in the body of the cope are *church window* hexagons of black, red, green and white satin, brocades and velvet; the orphrey is made of crimson velvet and gold octagons and squares and the hood is in a pattern of crimson velvet and green and white satin, incorporating a cross in the arrangement of the patches. The morse is in a diamond check of red velvet and white brocade squares. The hood, morse and orphrey are geometrical in pattern, in contrast to the shaded colouring of the rest of the work. Hidden within the lining of fine green glazed cotton is an embroidered panel of linen, recording the names of the workers, the date and the purpose of the work. Stoles of patchwork are occasionally found, but it is surprising how few church vestments have been made of patchwork. Heavy brocades and satins, especially those with woven metallic threads, are not suitable for many household furnishings, but are appropriate and effective in any article used on ceremonial occasions.

Coverlets were not numerous, although a few were made during the war, but since 1945 they have become popular again, the notable difference from the older fashions being that the majority are made in smaller sizes for beds which now measure considerably less than those of two hundred years ago; instead of the eleven feet of those days, a modern bed averages about three feet in width. This means that less work is entailed, but even so most large pieces of patchwork, such as coverlets and curtains, are made by a number of people working together. Members of Women's Institutes, Townswomen's Guilds, societies interested solely in needlework and other organisations such as the Embroiderers' Guild, are particularly active in this way.

Patchwork is not generally made in schools, but where teachers themselves are interested, the younger children are often taught to make small articles. At Tudor Hall school near Banbury the children make patchwork coverlets and other smaller articles in weekly needlework classes which are part of the school curriculum. The headmistress, Miss Nesta Inglis, makes the designs and works with the children and the work is sold at an annual sale for school charities. The number of individual workers throughout the country must now be counted in many hundreds. Classes in country districts and schools of three or four days' duration, in residential colleges under the control of the local education authorities in many counties, are held especially for giving instruction in craft work; traditional patchwork is included among the subjects. The examples of contemporary work which are illustrated were all made after 1949, the earliest being the coverlet (*184*) which was completed in that year, to a given design, by Mrs Hill and Mrs Ralph of Backwell in Somerset; it was sold and in 1956 was loaned for an exhibition in Ottawa, as an example of contemporary English work. Another coverlet, loaned for the same exhibition, was a copy of the eighteenth-century strip pattern illustrated (*111*) and made by Mrs A. K. McCosh of Coulter in Scotland in 1956, of contemporary glazed cotton prints. The coverlet shown in Figure *186* is made of geometrically shaped pieces (hexagons) in an ungeometrical pattern and does not conform to the conventional type of pattern. The coloured patches are kept to the swags and garland of printed floral chintzes, except for a scattering of single, floral hexagon pieces in the ground. The white ground is made from a collection of linen, calico, piqué and marcella pieces, and is broken by a pattern made from lavender-spotted white cotton. Detail of the centre is shown in Figure *181*. The pincushion (*182*) and cushion cover (*183*) are in strictly geometrical and traditional patterns, and the shapes of the patches in the pincushion and of the pattern in the cushion are emphasised by the way in which the material designs have been used. The accuracy was assured by cutting out the patches with "A" templates of each shape (p. 36).

It is sad that the ways of patchwork and quilting have not continued to run closely side by side. Even in the early years of the nineteenth century, when applied work coverlets were so much in fashion that the quilted covers were ousted from the top of the bed, patchwork was still used as a "top" for quilts. Nowadays the quilters who are upholding the tradition of their craft do not practise it on patchwork and most of the women who make patchwork do not possess the necessary knowledge, skill or equipment to quilt their work. A small number of unpadded coverlets have a line of running stitches round the outline of some patches or parts of the colour pattern but, generally speaking, this is now done as a means of attaching the lining to the patchwork top without an interlining and in no way compares with the decorative patterns on the true quilts. Knotting or tying (p. 89) has taken its place to a great extent and is sufficient to keep in place a flat interlining, such as domette, flannel or blanket.

Patchwork in the 1950s has not yet achieved the gentle elegance and precision of the applied and mosaic patterns of the early 1800s, nor has it sunk to the second-rate gentility of a hundred years ago, which indulged in fussy detail and set its pins and needles into over-elaborate *crazy* work or more intricate patterns. It is in the process of shaking off bad habits acquired in the war-years of stress and hasty economy, and getting down to shaping its contemporary character with materials (especially cottons) which are good and plentiful enough to be cheap;

181 *Detail of the centre pattern on fig. 186. The pattern is made of printed cottons with no embroidery.*
Designed and made by Averil Colby

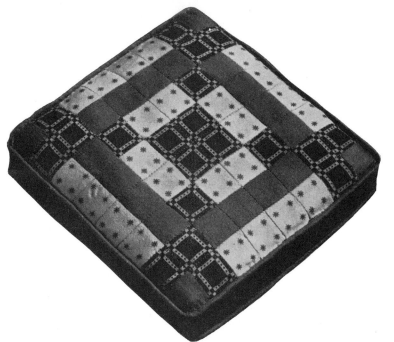

182 *A pincushion of contemporary cottons in red and white dress prints. 1951. Designed and made by Averil Colby*

183 *A cushion cover in traditional hexagon and diamond star pattern of contemporary cottons in shades of grey, white and black known as Black Frost. 1953. Designed and made by Averil Colby*

184 *A star-patterned coverlet in red, blue and white cotton hexagons, with small star shapes in diamond patches of dark blue. The Milky Way is a contemporary name for this pattern. 1949. Designed by Averil Colby*

185 *A cope in velvet and satin made to commemorate the coronation of Queen Elizabeth II by the parishioners of Burford, Oxfordshire, 1954. Designed by Averil Colby*

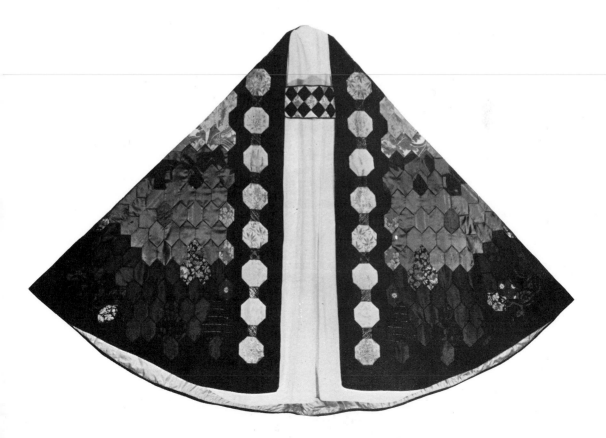

186 *A cotton coverlet of hexagons in an unconventional pattern made of nineteenth-and twentieth-century floral chintzes in a white ground. High Summer is a contemporary name for this design. Completed 1951. Designed and made by Averil Colby*

in spite of the temptation of inexpensive ready-made clothes in the shops, home dressmaking still flourishes and provides an ample supply of cuttings for patch-work. Chair covers and other small furnishings are also made at home of gay and appropriate materials; retail shops and trade houses are willing to sell out-of-date patterns and workroom cuttings by the pound weight. The background setting for making patchwork is not unlike what it was when patterns were at their best, except that to-day's workers have a rich tradition upon which to build.

NOTES ON MAKING TEMPLATES

The making of home-made templates is much to be commended. Apart from the independence of being able to try out new shapes at will, as well as the obvious economy, there is virtue in maintaining a tradition and it is mainly for those who wish to be thus virtuous that some instructions for the making of simple templates are being given.

For this, a certain amount of special equipment and tools is needed, but these will depend on the materials used. Cardboard, zinc and aluminium can be cut comparatively easily by using strong scissors. Perspex needs a fine hacksaw, and any other metal, such as tin, brass and copper, can be cut with metal shears. Shears are also useful for the thicker gauges of aluminium and, for the benefit of left-handed workers, these may be bought with a right or left-hand "cut".

All the templates must be made with precision and accuracy, but, in particular, great care is needed with the templates from which the paper patterns will be cut. A small inaccuracy in the outline of these templates can throw out the fitting of the patches in mosaic patterns. For this reason also, templates which have been cut-out with scissors must be treated with a proper care when they are in use.

The basic tools which are needed for cutting all templates are:

> A pair of compasses and a protractor.
> Inch rule, preferably of metal, but otherwise wooden with a metal edge.
> A cutting board.
> A lino-cutting knife or a wood-chisel and hammer.
> Strong scissors.
> A consistently sharpened pencil.

In addition to these tools, a hack-saw or metal shears may be added when they are necessary.

To draw any regular polygon, divide the number of degrees in a circle by the number of sides. There being 360° in a circle, for a hexagon it is necessary to divide 360° by 6, which gives 60°; for a pentagon divide by 5, which gives an angle of 72°, and for an octagon, when divided by 8, the result is 45°.

GENERAL BASIS FOR POLYGONAL SHAPES

First draw a base line and then erect a perpendicular to this base. The centre of the polygon will be on this perpendicular.

Next select a suitable diameter (according to the size required for the template), half of which will be the radius.

Then with the radius draw a circle with the centre on the perpendicular, and the rim touching the base line.

FOR A HEXAGON

At the crossing of the base and perpendicular mark off an angle of half the required amount thus: 60° divided by 2 is 30°.

Where the 30° angle cuts the rim of the circle make a mark and set the compass to this from the first point. With this radius, next mark off a similar point on the opposite side.

Repeat this on each side, and, using the point where the perpendicular cuts the top of the circle, join the six points and a hexagon results.

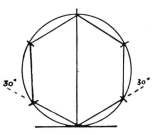

187   *Diagram for making a hexagon*

FOR A PENTAGON

Repeat the instructions for a general basis until the circle is drawn. Next, at the crossing of the base and the perpendicular mark off an angle of half the amount required thus: 72° divided by 2 gives 36°.

The distance between where the perpendicular cuts the circle is the length of one side, so with a compass mark off round the rim the remaining three points and a pentagon will result.

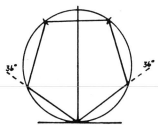

188   *Diagram for making a pentagon*

FOR AN OCTAGON

Repeat the instructions for a general basis until the circle is drawn. For an octagon the required angle is 45° which divided by 2 gives 22½°.

Mark off as for the other polygons to find the length of one **side**; repeat until the other seven points are marked and join them by straight lines, when a hexagon will be the result.

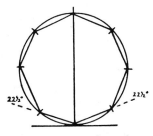

189   *Diagram for making an octagon*

FOR A DIAMOND SHAPE BASED ON A HEXAGON

The combination of diamond and hexagon shapes in one pattern is commonly used, but the side measurements must be identical in each shape.

Having made the hexagon to the required size, repeat the drawing and letter the six angle points, A, B, C, D, E, F (*190*).

Then join points A/D and B/E and the resulting two diamond and two half-diamond (or triangular) segments will fit the original hexagon and can be joined with it in making patterns.

Another method of making the same diamond shape shows the construction of the *box* pattern, in which three diamonds are joined to make a hexagonal outline. Still

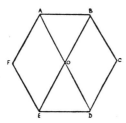

190 *Diamonds and half-diamonds made from a hexagon*

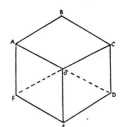

191 *Construction of the box pattern*

using the hexagon shape as the starting point, letter the six points as before A, B, C, D, E, F, and also the centre of the hexagon, on the spot made by the point of the compasses; this is marked with the letter O.

Next join each *alternate* angle point with the centre point O—for example A/O, C/O, E/O, and the original hexagon will be seen to consist of three identical diamond shapes.

TO MAKE A DIAMOND BASED ON A SQUARE

The simplest method is to begin by drawing an octagon.

So, begin by drawing an octagon in which the centre point is marked O, and the eight angle points A, B, C, D, E, F, G, H.

Next join points O/B and O/C; the measurement of each of these lines is equal to that of each of the four sides of the resulting diamond. Take a pair of compasses; with the distance equal to O/B and using B as the centre, describe an arc. Next, using C as the centre, describe another arc and mark the meeting point of both arcs as I. Next join B/I and C/I to complete the diamond.

This diamond may be used in pattern-making with a square, in which the measurement of each side is equal to that of each side of the diamond.

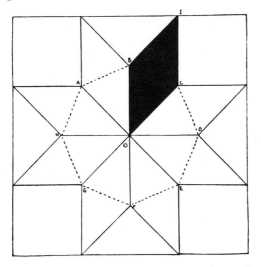

192　*Diagram for a long diamond to be used with a square*

NOTES ON MAKING AND JOINING GEOMETRICAL PATCHES

The traditional techniques employed in making geometrical shapes are still in use to-day, although the popularity of some processes has changed. For instance, it is now more usual to join prepared patches by seaming, rather than by the older and quicker method of running them together. Seaming is undoubtedly stronger and at one time was used only for unquilted work; also the urgent need for making a bed-cover of odd scraps has now gone, and without the urgency, so more care and consideration may be given to making and joining the patches with a precise and clear outline. This effect is achieved more successfully by seaming, than by running the patches together.

In this Appendix, in which the technical processes of preparing geometrical patches and then joining them together are explained, the different types of work are put under headings for convenience. Ways of doing applied work are given separately, in Appendix D.

Tradition allows of two methods in joining patchwork pieces. The first is that in which the patches are prepared and then inlaid and joined on the back of the work in two ways:

(i) By *seaming*, after the patches have been prepared by tacking the material over paper patterns, as in hexagons, etc.

(ii) By *running*, after the patches have been cut out only and have no prepared hem, as in square patches, etc.

The second method for joining patches is that in which the shapes are laid with their edges overlapping and are joined on the *face* of the work in three ways:

(i) By running stitch on the raw edges of the trimmed patches, which are then further sewn with embroidery over the running, as in *Crazy* patchwork.

(ii) By running on the raw edge of measured strips, which are folded back over the stitches, as in *Log-cabin*.

(iii) By hemming the prepared patches into position in rows and on to the row of patches beneath, as in *Shell* patchwork.

These methods are very similar to those in applied work, but as the patches make up the fabric, they are closer to the mosaic type than the work which is only decorative. It is impossible to look on any one method as being absolutely cut and dried, as there are so many ways in which they have been adapted and carried out; the basic methods only are given, with notes on some of the variations, and the realisation that there are probably many more. There are, however, some general practices which do not alter very much.

THE PAPER PATTERNS

The cutting-out of paper patterns is an important part of patchwork and a template should always be used. The shape and size of the papers determine the proportions of each patch and inaccurate cutting spoils the good fitting when they are joined together.

All the papers of a similar shape in one piece of work must be identical in size and shape. The even thickness of the paper is important; two papers instead of one in the patches of a section of work will enlarge the patches and also the section, so that it will not fit into the rest of the work. Cutting the papers may be rather a tedious business but they are the foundation of the precision in patchwork.

They should be cut with scissors, and from not more than two thicknesses of paper at a time; the scissors should hug the edge of the template with each cut. It is *not* a good thing to pencil the outline and then cut out along it; the lines thicken with the blunting of the pencil and the result is inaccurate and unreliable patterns. Paper will destroy the cutting edge of scissors and it is advisable to keep a pair especially for this. A separate template is needed also, for each shape used.

CUTTING OUT MATERIALS

There does not seem to have been any traditional or accepted method of cutting out materials with accuracy until the introduction of the "window" template about 1930. Before this the paper patterns previously cut from a basic shape were pinned or held on to the material and the shapes cut out with allowances made for turnings as the cutting proceeded. This method has not died out entirely to-day but the use of the "window" template is becoming more general with increasingly good results in the patchwork being done.

The comparatively careful method of cutting round a paper shape was only confined to the best examples of work. A more happy-go-lucky way was to fold over any piece of material large enough to cover the paper and to leave the surplus turnings untrimmed at the back of the work, which was clumsy and wasteful of material.

In many quilts, however, the skill and accuracy with which the patches have been cut make it obvious that, as with all traditional crafts handed down by word of mouth and example, patchwork improved or deteriorated according to the individual worker. A good technique was evolved and handed down by the master hand and inaccurate and untidy work was produced by someone of a different temperament.

The good wearing of any patchwork relies on the proper use and cutting of the material. In cutting out patches of any shape there are two points to consider:

(i) That the printed or woven pattern is used to its best advantage in building up the design of the patchwork.

(ii) That as far as possible the patches are cut with regard to the warp of the material. The fullest use should be made of the "pull" of the fabric, i.e. the way in which the warp threads run; this is indicated by the selvedge on all woven materials.

In fragments in which the selvedge is absent it is often difficult to decide in which way the pull of the material lies. A simple way to find out is to hold a piece between the thumb and forefinger of each hand, approximately two to three inches apart, and then to jerk or pull sharply at the material, first in one direction of the weave and then in directly the opposite way. The sound made by the material in response to this treatment will be on a noticeably higher note in one direction, which indicates the way in which the selvedge runs.

It is a good working principle that the threads of the material should follow the same direction in as many patches as possible. This applies particularly when patches of a plain or neutral colour are being assembled as a background for a design in colours or patterned material. If the principle is followed through in the joining of the patches as well as in the cutting, the resulting patchwork will be stronger than if it had been unplanned. There are inevitable exceptions to every rule, and when only small fragments are available for cutting it is of more importance that they are not wasted than that pieces should be discarded simply because the thread does not run in a certain direction for the patch.

The pattern of the finished work must also be considered and for this, also, it may be better on occasions to concentrate on the colour or pattern of the fabric, rather than on the weave. The various shapes have different points to look for in cutting out and these are given in the relevant paragraphs later in this appendix. There are, however, some methods which are general in cutting out, especially in the use of templates in pairs, and the resulting economy of material with the "A" template (*2*) used in conjunction with the corresponding "B" (*3*) for papers. The width of the frame in "A" regulates the amount of turning necessary for use with its partner shape "B".

The cutting-out of the fabric patches may be done by holding template A (*193*) directly on to the material, on the *right* side, and cutting with sharp scissors round the outside edge of the shape. Alternatively, a good method is to place the material, with the *wrong* side uppermost, on some hard surface (such as a cutting board) and mark the outline of the shape with a sharp pencil. The advantage of this method is that if a mistake is made, the material is not marked and spoiled for use, which would be the case if a mistake occurred when marking out on the face of the fabric. It should be pointed out, however, that this method can be followed on patterned materials only when the pattern is sufficiently visible on the wrong side.

The second method is of assistance to the inexperienced, although it is scorned by some of the "old hands" who are sure of themselves. However, there is much to be said for the old saying that it is "better to be safe than sorry" and especially when working with pieces that are precious and scarce it is better to pencil a piece before it is cut. (Note: a white pencil is good for use on dark materials.) It is not possible to stress too much the importance of the good-wearing quality when selecting materials, especially in those which have been used. Before cutting used materials, they should be inspected carefully for thin or badly worn places. A quick way to detect this is to hold the material against a window-pane in daylight, when any flaws and weaknesses will show at once. These should be clearly marked with a pencil line, leaving a good clearance area round the unwanted pieces. They will then be easy to avoid when cutting out. Care should also be taken to avoid the holes in the trade patterns which have been held together in swags or books by pins or metal clips.

TACKING

Tacking or basting stitches should not be overdone. They are intended only as a temporary measure to keep the patches in shape or position until they are stitched together and are later removed. They should of course be sufficiently adequate to keep a hem firmly in place; no backstitching or cross tacking is necessary when covering papers. In covering patterns with material, it is generally sufficient to take one tacking stitch for each turning of the hem; large-size patches may need more. One stitch should be made in the centre of each hem, with the thread taken *over* the fold of material at the corners (*194, 197*). It will be found that this will contain the fold neatly and that there is no need for a backstitch.

The tacking in some work of the nineteenth century consisted of stitching taken from side to side on the back of each patch, crossing and recrossing over the paper pattern. It is also a method given for some American patchwork at the present time, but it seems to be no more effective and requires more time and work than the simpler and quicker way of tacking round the hem of the patches only.

As a further note on tacking, it is an advantage to omit making a knot in the thread, and for a good reason: after the joining of the patches has been completed, all the tacking threads and paper patterns are removed; this stage of the work is simplified and speeded up if the threads can be withdrawn easily and without the hindrance of knots or backstitching. An additional advantage is that the work does not become creased and untidy, which is apt to occur during the removing of the papers if due care is not taken.

The proper understanding and handling of materials comes with experience, but one or two observations which apply to most materials may usefully be made here in connection with the methods of tacking.

All fabrics with a delicate surface texture, such as glazed cottons, silks, satins and so on, need particular care so that the surface is not marred by pin or needle pricks. Marks like these will spoil the appearance of the patches and cannot be obliterated successfully, unless the work is washed. In this case any fabric with a surface glaze loses its character and with it much of its freshness of appearance.

Unglazed cotton materials are not so badly affected by pin-marks, but it is always noticeable where care has not been taken to avoid surface pricks. Velvet retains the mark of a tacking stitch where the pile has been pressed down by the thread, although the pile hides the prick marks made by pins or needles more successfully than smoother fabrics. The difficulty in handling velvet is in its tendency to "creep." It is possible to overcome this by allowing a wider hem than is usually given by an "A" template. This allows for the "take-up" in the turning of the material over the paper pattern. It does not make very much difference to the depth of hem on the back of the work, but is sufficient to hold the tacking. The difficulty of making a hem for velvet patches was probably one reason for its popularity in crazy patchwork, in which no turnings are necessary. It should be appreciated, also, that greater skill is needed in using velvet for geometrical shapes.

As it is well to make an effort to preserve the face of the work free from unnecessary prick marks, all pinning and stitching should be kept to the back of the patches wherever possible. In some shapes the technique of joining calls for surface stitching, but in most work it is confined to the back. If the tacking stitches which hold down the hem catch only the hem and the paper pattern, without being taken through to the front of each patch, all the prick marks will be avoided.

In preparing the patches for Shell patchwork this is not such a simple problem, as paper patterns are not used for this shape (p. 176). It is possible, however, when handling chintz in Shell patchwork, to hold the folded hem in place by lightly tacking the hem only and not stitching through to the front of the patch.

It is important also to refrain from pinning any materials which will show the marks afterwards; or at any rate they should be pinned where the marks will not be noticed.

GENERAL NOTES ON THE PREPARATION OF PATCHES

Although the preparation of the patches for joining may be the least interesting part of patchwork, its importance is obvious. The correct and careful cutting and tacking together of material and paper pattern is the basis of good construction. The use of paper patterns is not an absolute necessity, but it has undoubted advantages. Providing the papers are carefully cut, they ensure accuracy and regulate the shapes which are used. This is especially so in making small-sized patches which are, perhaps surprisingly, the most difficult to make with necessary neatness and precision.

Patches of different shapes can be combined to make a pattern in one piece of work, as long as the measurement of the sides in each shape are identical. Notes on the construction of different shapes are given later in this chapter.

In the practice of construction and joining of all shapes in patchwork, it must be remembered that no trick or sleight of hand or "wangling" can correct an ill-prepared patch. It must be remade. One irregular or badly-shaped patch can throw out a pattern and spoil a design.

There is no rule of thumb about the spacing of the stitches along the joins of the patches. The seams especially should be drawn together closely, particularly at the corners; hemming and running stitches should be even, and the amount of material which is taken up in each stitch should be equal to the space between them. The number of stitches to the inch should vary from sixteen to twenty-four, according to the thickness of the material—velvet will probably need sixteen or eighteen and a fine chintz from twenty to twenty-four to the inch.

HEXAGONS

A template is needed for cutting-out all the various six-sided shapes. Although only the equilateral hexagon—the *Honeycomb*—is shown in the stages of preparation the method used is the same for other shapes (such as the *octagon*), in which the corner angles are wider than a right angle. Hexagonal shapes which are not equilateral have probably developed from the basic shape through guess-work methods of cutting the paper patterns. When only card templates were used, they gradually lost their original shape in the process of cutting-out. Small shavings off the sides and consequent trimming "to get it right" eventually resulted in a patch which could only be described as a first cousin to the original, but which could be used to build up a good patchwork pattern, nevertheless.

No doubt, also, an individual worker, wanting to "go one better" than her neighbour, has from time to time evolved a variation of the pattern, and in time it has become one of the number of traditional shapes.

The *Church Window* shape is a hexagon. It is an interesting shape to use, either by itself or with squares (*14, 15*) or other shapes. The shape obviously got its name by reason

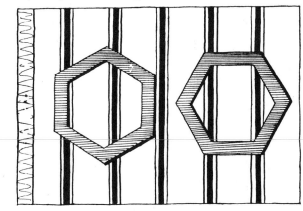

193   *Cutting material and designing with hexagon*
"A" (window) template

of its resemblance to the Early English (Gothic) church window. The *Coffin* (*13*) also because of its resemblance to, but not because of its association with, this mournful object.

On second thoughts, and remembering the story of the Brereton hangings (p. 109), perhaps this is not altogether so. No mention is made of either of these two shapes by name in any patchwork, other than English. The *Coffin* does not appear to have been much used. The example shown in the Brereton bed furnishings (*121*) is the only large piece of work in the shape, although smaller things, such as cushion covers and button-bags, were occasionally made. There is a small fragment also in the Victoria and Albert Museum.

The *Honeycomb* has been a universally favourite pattern, especially for quilts, for at least two hundred years and it is to be found in most of the patchwork in this country.

To many people the shape itself means patchwork and for this reason it is being used in this book as the basic shape for the process which applies to many mosaic patterns such as the *octagon* and other shapes. The templates used are shown (*2, 3*) and are referred to in the relative stages of the work with diagrams to illustrate all the processes.

To make *Honeycomb* patchwork:

(i) A number of *paper patterns* are cut from template "B" (*3*).

(ii) Using template "A" (*2*) a number of *patches* are cut also in material. (In cutting hexagon patches with regard to the weave of the material, two sides of the template should bisect the warp or alternatively they should be parallel with it (*193*).

(iii) A *paper pattern* is placed in the centre and on the *wrong side* of each patch. The paper and patch may be pinned together at this stage to facilitate handling, but this is not a good thing to do when the material is glazed.

(iv) The patch is held with the attached paper uppermost and the hem on each side is then turned over and tacked on to the paper (*194*). One tacking stitch is made in the centre of each side and the thread taken over the fold at each corner, as shown in the diagram. The thread should be drawn with a firm tension and finished off by running an extra stitch into the first turning. Cut off the thread, to leave an end of about one-

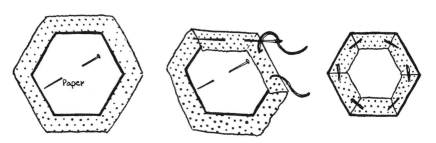

194   *Preparing a hexagon patch*

quarter of an inch. This should hold the thread until such time as it must be withdrawn. There is no need for a backstitch, in fact this would be a nuisance as well as being unnecessary.

The patches are then ready for joining.

(v) A number of prepared patches should be arranged in a pattern, face uppermost, preparatory to joining them together.

(vi) Patches are joined by holding them face to face, the edges neatly together and with the wrong sides outwards, and stitching by seaming or top-sewing (*195*).

It is important that the stitches be evenly spaced, but not in any way crowded. A seam too closely stitched can be a weakness, as the stitches then allow for no "give" and are also inclined to split the threads of the material.

The seaming should begin at the extreme end of each seam and continue for the full length of it. This is important. Any part of the seam which is not stitched results in a gap which is noticeable from the front of the work. This is not only unsightly, but is a weakness in the construction.

The beginning of the thread is secured by "sewing-in" about a quarter of an inch, thus avoiding the use of a knot. To end the seam, the thread is sewn back for three or four stitches and cut off.

It will not be necessary to end-off the thread for every short seam; indeed the work is stronger with as few joins in the thread as possible, and with a little forethought in planning this joining can be reduced to a minimum.

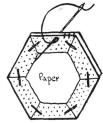

(vii) When, eventually, the pieces are all sewn together, the work should be placed face downwards on a flat surface and the tacking threads withdrawn so that the paper patterns may be lifted out. It is here that the benefit of omitting knots and back-stitching comes in, and this somewhat tedious process is much speeded up without their hindrance.

195 *Seaming two hexagons together*

When the tacking has been removed, it *is* possible to shake out the used papers, but this is not really satisfactory. Some papers are invariably left in and if they are not found and taken out, they will "ball" when washed and make hard lumps inside the work.

DIAMONDS

The diamond patch—and indeed any shape in which there are any sharply-angled corners—requires a greater degree of skill to prepare than in making hexagonal, octagonal or similar patches. Others which need the same treatment as the diamond are triangles and some pentagonal shapes (*28, 29*). The difficulty comes in disposing of the folds of material at the pointed ends. The emphasis of the pattern is in the clear precision of the diamond points—particularly so if the shapes are joined in star-fashion. If the ends are blunted at all, the character of the shape is lost. Used in conjunction with hexagons, it can relieve a somewhat monotonous *Rosette* pattern or it can dominate the design as when it is used in the "Milky Way" (*184*) and "Black Frost" (*183*).

Used alone, the diamond unit is the foundation of the "Box Pattern" (*19*).

The two *Diamonds* most consistently used are those based on the hexagon (*18*) and on the square (*23*), but there are several variations. One is that in which the diamond is nearly but not quite square. In others (*24*) the sides in one half of each shape have been shortened, so that the patch almost resembles a kite. These two last diamonds are used together to produce the two *double-star* patterns (*25, 26*).

The same method for paper-cutting is applied to diamond patterns as to all other shapes in which they are used (p. 165). It is, perhaps, not quite such a carefree operation in this case, as here particular attention must be given at the pointed ends of the shape, to see that the exact angle is maintained in each pattern.

Any failure in this can spoil the finished design of the work.

171

TO MAKE A DIAMOND PATCH

(i) A number of *paper patterns* are cut from template "B" (5).

(ii) Using template "A" (4) a number of patches are cut from material. To be successful the material used should only be that which is reasonably firm and of even weave and texture. Any material which "slips" or "creeps" needs a skilful hand to work it and even so the result is not always good. Velvet is particularly difficult to handle and present-day rayons unspeakably so. First-quality cottons and the fine linens are the most adaptable to the processes of preparing and fitting the patches. Any material which lends itself well, and will keep a fold when pressed with the hand while working, is the best for negotiating the worst corners.

Before the days of templates, cutting the material accurately for diamond shapes presented no great problem. The material was cut on the bias, in measured strips of

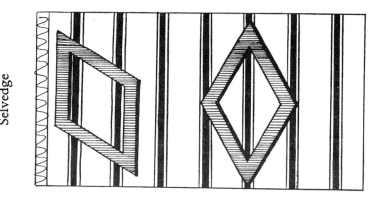

Selvedge

196 *Cutting material and designing with diamond "A"*
(window template)

even width. The strips were then cut into measured sections, using the thread of the material as a cutting line. There is no reason why this method should not still be used, providing the material is in large enough pieces to be worth while. It might not be a satisfactory way in which to cut for design, but it is quite suitable for white or plain-coloured materials. The only method given here in the diagram is with the use of a template.

There are two schools of thought as to the way in which the patches should be cut, with regard to the warp of the material. It will be seen from the diagram (*196*) that one way of cutting shows the straight edge of the template "A" lying on the selvedge line, whereas in the other position the "way" of the material runs from point to point. In the first position the patches have the advantage of two sides on the "straight", but in the second all four sides are cut on the bias of the material.

(iii) A paper pattern is placed on the wrong side of the patch, as for the hexagon, and the same care taken with pinning the two together.

(iv) The patch is held with the attached paper uppermost and in the position shown in the diagram (*197*). Beginning with the hem on the right of the top point, this side is the first to be tacked down.

(v) The corner is then mitred by folding down the hem at the point, so that the

197   Preparing a diamond patch

fold lies parallel to the edge of the paper pattern but does not overlap it. This fold is not stitched until the next hem is turned in.

(vi) The second hem is next turned and tacked down.

The process is repeated for the other two sides to complete the tacking of the patch.

When a number of patches have been prepared and arranged in a pattern they are seamed together (*198*) as they are arranged and with the same processes as are given for hexagon patches.

Although the seaming is a straightforward process, the joining of diamond patches together in a *Star Pattern* is not always as simple as it seems to make sure that the points fit well in the centre of each star.

It is a good plan to stitch each seam from the "shoulder" of the patches towards the point (*198*). In this way the material is gradually worked towards the centre of the star, where

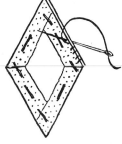

198   Seaming two diamonds together

there is liable to be a slight hole or gap, if the mitred corners have not been altogether successful. With a small amount of material, the worker is able to cover her tracks, but the gap should in no case be filled by "cobbling".

BRICK PATTERN AND SQUARES

The rectangular shape of the pieces used in the brick-pattern is straightforward; the thread of the material is generally used as a guide for cutting along the necessary straight lines. The process of cutting-out can be simplified even more, if swags of trade samples or ready-cut patterns of cloth are used. There appears to be no standard measurement or size for them, but if one can judge by the pieces in old quilts, the proportion of a "brick" was usually on the basis of the length being twice that of its width. It is perhaps of interest to note here the classical measurement of the rectangle. The early Greek architects based all design on geometrical proportion and gave that of the perfect rectangle as being 1 by 1·68. This would be a good basis for the proportion of "bricks".

The ready-cut patterns of a convenient size to use in "brick" patchwork are obtainable generally in dress and shirting fabrics in cottons, cotton poplins and the like; otherwise lengths and pieces of similar materials are reduced to the right size and shape by cutting them into strips and then by dividing the strips into measured lengths, according to the size of the proposed "bricks".

Neither template nor paper patterns are needed for this shape, although they are an advantage when used for small patches, which are more difficult to make accurately without a paper pattern.

TO MAKE BRICKS AND SQUARES

The preparation of the patches depends on the method to be used in joining. There are two orthodox ways of doing this.

The oldest, and most usual, requires no preparation of the "brick" patches other than the cutting out. Two "bricks" are placed together with the wrong sides of the material outermost and they are joined carefully, with a running stitch, about a quarter of an inch in from the raw edges. It is important that the stitches be neat and not too long.

The second, and most satisfactory way, is to prepare each patch by turning down, to the wrong side of the material, a small hem of not more than a quarter of an inch on each of the four sides. The "bricks" are then joined by a seaming stitch, worked on the wrong side.

The emphasis in the building of the pattern is on the use of contrasts. The "bricks" should be sorted into contrasting shades of colours or patterns, such as light and dark shades of any colour, or into plain and patterned materials, or into white or coloured pieces, as in the quilt in brick pattern which is illustrated (146). When joining the "bricks", those of contrasting colours are placed alternately in strips the length of the quilt and when sufficient strips have been completed they, in turn, are joined and arranged so that, again, contrasting colours or patterns fall together.

In the variation of the pattern known as the *Brick Wall,* the rows are joined across the width of the quilt, with every alternate row beginning and ending with a "half-brick". By thus breaking the vertical lines of the brick pattern, the resulting design gives an effect of a brick wall. This is sometimes varied again by the addition of "cement" or strips of white calico between the bricks (179).

In the *Brick* pattern the rectangular patch is used to make an all-over patterned quilt, but it can also be used in conjunction with a square patch. In this case the two shapes must be in correct proportion one to the other—the rectangle being the same width but twice the length of the square. Particular care is needed, when making the square patches, to see that the four sides are the same length and that the corners are strictly right-angled. No other shape in patchwork can be so obviously "off-true" as an inaccurately made square.

NOTES ON MAKING SHELL, LOG-CABIN AND CRAZY WORK

The *shell* pattern is the only one of the three types of patchwork in this chapter which has a geometrical shape and for which a template is needed. It has two alternative names; *fish-scale* is one by which it is known in England and apparently not elsewhere; *clam-shell* is a name used here and in America, but it is commonly known in England as *shell*. The pattern outline is familiar and is made on the principle of overlapping circles, in which it appears that two concave quarter-segments have been cut away from a circle, leaving a convex semicircular outline on one side tapering to a narrow point on the opposite edge. As one of the all-over designs in patchwork, the effect depends on the emphasis given to the outline of each patch by the use of clear contrasting colours. The patches are joined, traditionally, in straight rows, but a recent method of joining in which this procedure is not followed is described after the two older traditional methods.

Shell patchwork is often included under the heading of appliqué, but it should be studied, more correctly, in a class by itself; although the patches are joined on the surface as for applied patterns, they do not rely on a foundation but the fabric is constructed from them. There seem to have been two ways of preparing the patches in the past. One in which the pattern is cut from a stiffened material (such as linen) and left in the patches as part of the completed work, and the other in which patches are shaped from a card pattern, which is afterwards removed.

The last, described as Method One, is the one most commonly used.

TO MAKE SHELL PATTERN—METHOD ONE

(i) Using a "B" template a number of thin card patterns are cut. The card should be slightly pliable and about the thickness of a postcard; it should in no way be stiff.

The template is placed on the card and, with a sharp pencil, a line is drawn round the outline. The pattern is then cut out from this line. (Note: this is contrary to the practice for cutting papers, for which it should never be used.)

It is well that a good number of card patterns are cut, according to the size of the work in hand, although the quantity needed is not to be compared with the number of papers used for other mosaic shapes.

Each card pattern may be used many times.

(ii) Using an "A" template a number of patches in material are cut. Here, also, a pencilled outline may be used as a guide for cutting, but as a precaution against mistakes it is usual to draw on the reverse side of the material, providing that the design is clearly enough seen.

It is important that all the patches are cut on the straight, with the points of the shells following the warp threads. It is incorrect to cut the patches in this shape other than on the straight of the material · the patches otherwise will tend to pull out of shape and will not lie flat, as they should do. The "pull" of each patch affects that of the completed work, in this more than in the angular shapes, owing to the curved edges of the patches being largely on the "cross" of the material.

(iii) A card pattern is pinned to the face of a patch (the right side of the material), so that it is exactly in the centre. Two pins are an advantage here, put in diagonally as they are shown in the diagram (*199*), so that they hold the material more firmly than if they are put in straight with the cloth.

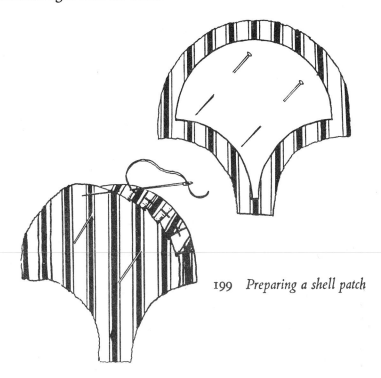

199 *Preparing a shell patch*

Besides being more secure, the patch is easier to handle, as the pinpoints lie in the same direction as the needle when working.

When glazed or delicate material is being used, the patch and card are pinned together at the point but with one pin only, so that any prick marks are less noticeable than in the main part of the patch. With experience, the pins may be omitted altogether.

(iv) The patch is next turned over with the material uppermost and, using the card pattern *as a guide only*, a hem is turned down on the wrong side, following exactly the shape of the pattern. The convex side only is hemmed; the two concave edges are left unhemmed, as this area on each patch provides the surface to which the next row of patches is stitched.

177

It is necessary that the fullness of the hem is taken-up neatly and this is achieved by pleated folds and *not by gathering*. Tacking stitches are made at short intervals to keep the pleats in place and the thread brought over each pleat as in the corner folds of other shapes.

The patch is *not* sewn on to the card pattern.

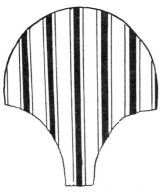

200   *A finished patch*

(v) The pins and card are removed when the hem is tacked and the process repeated until sufficient patches are made to complete the first two rows across the width of the curtain, coverlet or whatever is being made.

One card pattern is re-used until it becomes too soft to continue; if the pins are replaced in the same holes each time, the life of the card is prolonged. It should survive the making of twenty or thirty patches at least and probably many more.

(vi) To join the patches: The first row of prepared patches is laid down on a flat surface. (Note: for this purpose, a cork bath-mat will be found especially useful. Pins can be put into it with ease and with no harm to the cork.) The top of each patch should lie against a straight line (such as a ruler) and the sides of it just touch those of its neighbours (*201*).

(vii) The patches for the second row are next laid in position. These should overlap

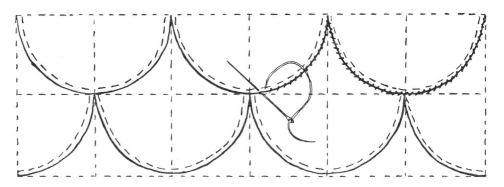

201   *Shell patches tacked round the curved edges for hemming. Dotted lines indicate guiding lines for placing the patches*

the patches in the first row by the depth of their hems about a quarter of an inch and lie on the unhemmed edges of the under-row of patches.

The centre of each second-row patch should come where the two under-patches meet. The amount of material which is left uncovered should correspond with the size of the basic pattern (template "B"). This is checked by placing template "B" on each under-patch in turn, before the patches in each succeeding row are finally pinned into position.

(viii) With the second row pinned to the patches in the first row, they are then both tacked together.

(ix) The final joining is done by hemming, on the front of the work. The stitches should be neat and continue round the semicircular hem on each patch to where the next patch touches.

Each row is completely finished as the work progresses. This includes, as well as

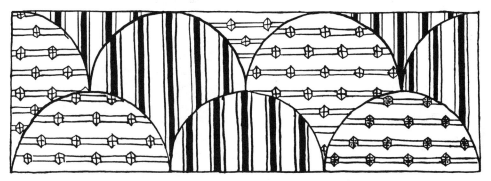

202   *Shell patches when joined showing smooth curves and neat fitting*

the hemming, the removal of all tacking threads and is done before the succeeding row is pinned into position.

The whole process is then repeated until enough rows have been joined to complete the work.

The traditional pattern of *Shell* patchwork should resemble the scales of a fish, each patch smoothly overlapping the patches on which it lies. The curved shapes give the work its character and it is here that the emphasis should be made. The first preparation of the hems must result in smooth curves, with no "pokes" to show where too large a pleat has been made, and the final hemming should be delicate and even—a test of skill and finesse. An irregular stitch is painfully apparent.

There is no great scope for variety in the traditional arrangement of the patches, but the shape itself is graceful and an invitation and a challenge to enterprise in colour.

TO MAKE SHELL PATTERN—METHOD TWO

(i) Using a template "B", a number of patterns are cut from some stiffened material, such as tailor's canvas, glazed calico or similar stuffs. The same method for cutting is used as for the card patterns, but enough patterns are needed to allow one for each patch.

(ii) Using a template "A", a number of patches are cut, as described on p. 176.

(iii) A canvas pattern is placed exactly in the centre of each patch, on the *wrong* side and fixed by pinning, in the same way as Method One.

(iv) The patch is held in the hand with the canvas uppermost and the hem is turned over the canvas, with the process of pleating and tacking followed as in Method One (p. 177). In this case the hem may be tacked on to the canvas, but in no case should it penetrate to the face of the patch.

(v) The pins are removed when the tacking is completed, but not the tacking threads or the canvas pattern, both of which remain in the patches.

(vi) The patches are placed in rows and joined by the same processes which are given in Method One.

It is obvious that work in which the canvas patterns remain is considerably heavier than that made with the guidance of card patterns and is suitable only for such things as curtains, where the extra thickness and weight may be an advantage.

In contemporary work it has been used for a small tea-cosy, in which instance it fulfils a useful function. But in a bed coverlet, where lightness and warmth are needed, the canvas patterns would, in effect, defeat this end in what would be a stiff and weighty piece of work.

The illustration shows a section of a hanging in the Victoria and Albert Museum (*113*). This is one of a pair of curtains made as a bed furnishing in which the canvas patterns still remain in the patches.

As in most patchwork, it is necessary to straighten the uneven edges before a lining can be attached. To do this at the ends of the work, it is usual to cut off the tops of the patches in the first row horizontally, and with these half-patches to fill in the spaces in the last row (*201*).

The side patches are given the same kind of treatment. The half of the end patch in each alternate row along one side is cut vertically and the halves used to fill in the spaces on the opposite side.

This activity is not as difficult to carry out as it appears to be and will be an obvious manœuvre when the appropriate moment, in fact, arrives.

As an alternative to cutting-off the half-patches, it is not incorrect to turn in the unwanted halves at the ends and sides of the work, but it is a considerable saving of material to make use of them.

At this stage, ways and means of lining and finishing are the same as for any other patchwork and can be carried out in whatever manner is in keeping with the general design. (See chapter on Lining and Finishing.)

TO MAKE SHELL PATTERN—METHOD THREE

Mention is made at the beginning of this section of yet another method in which the patches are inlaid. Here, the patches are prepared as for the angular shapes, in that a hem is turned down on all sides of the patches and not on one side only as in Method One and Two in this shape.

Using template "B", the patterns are cut from very thin card or stiff paper. Each is covered with a patch cut from template "A". The convex edges have the hems pleated in the conventional way: the concave edges must have the hem "nicked" lightly to ease the material round the curves.

203   *Arrangement of inset shell patches*

The shells are then arranged to form a pattern, not overlapping but with convex and concave edges inset, one within the other, giving a smooth surface to the work (*203*).

The edges are joined by a close slip-stitch, in which the stitches are not visible on the right side.

LOG-CABIN

The Log-cabin type of patchwork is (like *shell* and *crazy* patterns) in a class of its own. Several other names are given to this work in America, such as *Barn-raising* or *Straight Furrow*, according to the way in which the colours in the pattern are arranged; there is no difference in the way it is made. There are, however, two patterns which are made slightly differently. They are the *Pineapple* pattern (*176*)—which is common to English and American work—and the "V" pattern, which seems to be known only on this side of the Atlantic.

Like *crazy* patchwork, *Log-cabin* is also sewn on to a foundation material, but each completed piece is a separate unit. The units are always square and the general design depends on the way in which the units are arranged.

The materials which have been used are generally thicker and rougher than most of the finer patterns. Tweeds and other woollen cloth, also silk, satin, cotton and velvet, have all been put together in one piece of work. A few quilts of *log-cabin* do show careful selection of materials and good results have come from using velvet or silk, or else a careful mixture of some silks, satins and velvets. The foundation carries some of the weight of the heavy materials, so that velvet does not drag so heavily on silk as it would do otherwise.

TO MAKE LOG-CABIN

(i) A square card is cut as a template for the foundation material. This is usually from twelve to fifteen inches square for a coverlet, and about six inches or less for smaller things such as cushions.

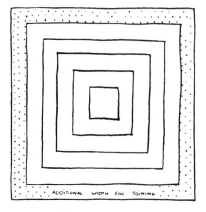

204 *Square card template ruled out with allowance marked for joining*

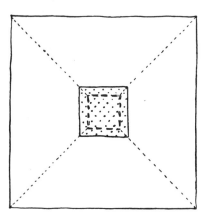

205 *Centre square of material tacked to the foundation*

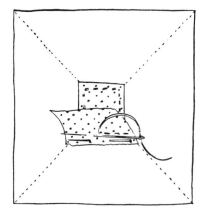

206 *First strip attached to the centre*

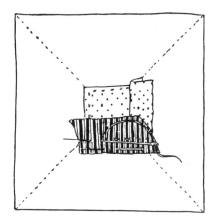

207 *Second strip sewn over the folded end of the first*

(ii) The template is then ruled out (*204*) so that the pieces of material needed can be measured. The number and width vary with the size of the square.

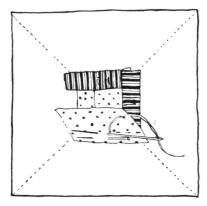

208 *Third and fourth strips in position*

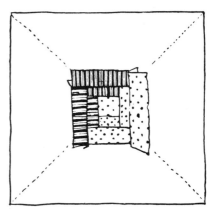

209 *Second row of strips in position*

(iii) A number of squares are cut out in foundation material, from the card template, leaving an allowance of about half an inch for joining. Sufficient squares are cut to complete the work on hand.

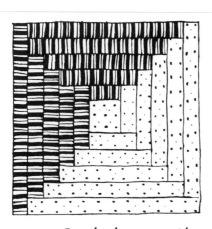

210 *Completed square with diagonal dividing line*

211 *One square of the "Pineapple" pattern*

(iv) A number of strips are cut, about one inch wide, of the materials to be used in the pattern. The lengths vary according to the measurements drawn on the card template; four strips of each length will be needed.

(v) Tacking stitches or crease marks are made diagonally from each corner of each foundation piece, so that they cross in the centre of the square. A square of material to be used in the pattern is stitched over the centre (*205*).

(vi) A short strip of material is first pinned and then sewn, about an eighth of an inch from the edge, covering one side of the centre square. When sewn it is folded back over the stitches and pressed down (*206*).

(vii) A second strip of material is pinned and tacked along the second side of the centre square, overlapping the first strip at one end (*207*).

(viii) The third and fourth sides of the centre square are covered at the edges by further strips of material, each strip overlapping the last at the end until the centre square is surrounded by strips (*208*).

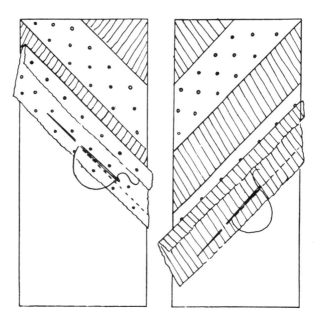

212 *Strips being sewn to lengths of calico for the*
"V" pattern

(ix) The process is repeated on the next round, this time the edges of the first rows of strips being covered (*209*), gradually building up the square until the whole of the foundation is covered (*210*). The final strip is folded over so that it meets the edges of the foundation. It is eventually hidden when the squares are joined together.

The pattern of *Log-cabin* depends on the arrangement of the light and dark shades in the coloured materials. The shading shown in the working diagrams is typical but there are several others, including squares which are built up of all light- or all dark-coloured strips.

To complete the work the squares are joined by backstitching on the wrong side. The general design depends on the relation of the light and dark sections in each square to those in adjoining squares; that is, whether two light-coloured sections touch one another or whether two dark sections come together. Two entirely different patterns are illustrated. Two of the American versions already mentioned are illustrated in Mrs Finley's *Old Patchwork Quilts*; *Barn-raising* and *Straight Furrow*.

The *Pineapple* pattern is made on the same principle as *Log-cabin*, but on every alternate journey around the square the strips are sewn across the corners diagonally (*211*).

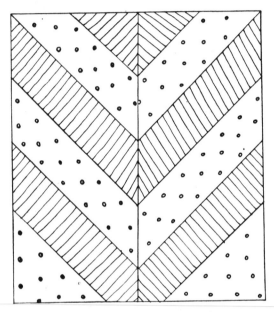

213   *Calico lengths joined with matching strips forming the "V" pattern*

It is the most effective when made in one colour with white; the coverlet illustrated is made of Turkey twill and white (*176*).

In the "V" pattern the strips of coloured materials are laid, stitched and folded in the same way as for *Log-cabin*, but they are sewn to narrow lengths of unbleached calico and the covered lengths are eventually joined to make up the coverlet (*212, 213*).

CRAZY PATCHWORK

The construction of Crazy patchwork does not require great skill in stitching or in planning a piece of work. Now, as in the past, any kind of material is used and almost invariably the pieces are those found in the dressmaker's rag-bag. The combining of many kinds of material is to the detriment of the work, and crazy work which has survived for any length of time has generally been carefully preserved. Anything which has been in regular use is in tatters and only kept for some reason such as sentimental or historical association.

The Victorian rage for this patchwork was encouraged by the large variety of silk and velvet used by the home dressmakers, but work done in the earlier years of the nineteenth century was more sturdy by nature and often included woollen pieces such as worsteds and suitings and was made into blankets and coverlets. Nowadays any work in this method is more often done with cotton materials. Unless a colour scheme is being considered, the work needs little or no planning beforehand. It is even possible to collect the pieces as the work proceeds and add them wherever there is a convenient place.

The preparation of the patches is simple. Any piece of material is taken, no matter what the shape, and cut to a convenient size with all the frayed edges and very irregular ends trimmed off. With a pile of pieces trimmed and prepared, the work is to arrange them on to a foundation of some material which is not too stiff, such as muslin, ticking, scrim or partly worn cotton sheeting, shirting or dress material. This foundation material may be in lengths which are seamed or run together to the size of the proposed piece

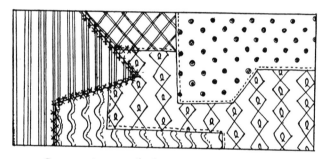

214 *Crazy pieces tacked in position with one piece herringboned over the tacking*

of work or it may consist of any odd pieces also joined to the required size. The foundation in Jenny Jones' quilt was cut into nine squares (*163*).

Each prepared patch is then laid on to the foundation (which should be perfectly flat), with the raw edges over- or under-lapping those of its neighbours to the depth of about half an inch. The first patch can be placed at any part of the foundation, but it is more convenient to begin at one corner; it should be sewn neatly down on the right side with a running stitch round the edges and the thread ended off firmly. The second patch is then sewn on in the same way, the stitches going through the material of the first patch where the two overlap, as well as through the underlying foundation. Pieces are added in this way until the whole of the foundation is covered when the patching is completed.

The next process is intended to hide the raw edges, as well as the running stitches, with a covering of embroidery (*214*). In the more modest pieces of work and where the probability of laundering would make it advisable, the embroidery is in either single, double or treble feather stitch, carried out in cotton thread, coarse embroidery silk or buttonhole twist. This addition has the advantage of strengthening, a little, the fabric of the work, but as all the stitching is done on the right side of the work it is subject to all the wear and tear in use and in consequence cannot greatly be relied upon to last for long. More elaborate stitches and patterns worked in richer threads are to be found on crazy work, especially on that done in the nineteenth century (*215*). There is no restraint shown in the number of patterns which can be worked or the different kinds of thread used in one article. Stars, hearts, kisses and shell shapes done in silk, silver and gold thread are lavished upon material often unable to carry the strain put upon it.

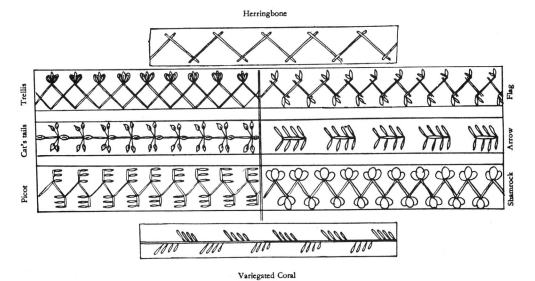

215   Stitches suitable for Crazy work given in Weldon's *Practical Publications in* 1885

Where elaborate embroidery is fancied, only firm material for the patches is any good and the choice of embroidery threads should be of the best. Cotton thread is used for the running stitches, generally size 40, 50 or 60 according to the general texture of the materials.

Although the patches are sewn to a foundation, this does not do away with the necessity of lining the work, except in such articles as cushion covers.

NOTES ON DOING APPLIED WORK

ONLAY

The technical importance of applied or "laid" work lies in the attachment of the superimposed pattern as smoothly and firmly as possible to the background material. The method of attaching is by simple stitchery, with the object of making sure that, in the ordinary course of wear and tear, it is impossible to detach the pattern. The cut edges of the materials must be covered so as to prevent fraying, and the stitches, which are used for joining and done on the face of the work, are designed to suit this purpose. The type of stitch and the colour of the thread can emphasise or soften the pattern outline in relation to the background; if a coloured pattern is applied to a white ground, its outline may be strengthened by the use of a close stitch—such as *button-hole* or *loop-stitch*—and a coloured thread; whereas an open stitch, such as *herringbone*, used with a white thread on a white ground, tends to merge the pattern into the background.

Simple embroidery stitches are included in applied work; they are found sometimes implementing a pattern, where the printed or woven colour or design on the material fails to carry it out successfully. Tradition allows of single lines of *stem-* or *chain-stitch* or occasional groups of stitches, to give emphasis to a detail—or to attach the centre of a large pattern more firmly when the outline stitch is insufficient. A good example of stitching implementing a pattern is seen in the features of the Lion receiving his name from Adam (*156*). Similarly a bird figure will sometimes have an embroidered eye or claws; the centre rib of a leaf or the outline of flower petals may be drawn with a line of stem-stitching, but the best tradition relies on applied pieces of fabric only for effect.

The need for good quality in material, and the avoidance of any fabric which will fray unduly, has already been mentioned in Chapter II. It is not possible to eliminate fraying altogether, but certain precautions can be taken to reduce it in the intricacies of applied work. A small amount of extra stiffening to the materials will control the tendency of the cut threads to spring out and become unravelled and a home-made paste can be used.

PASTE FOR APPLIED WORK

To make the paste pour less than half a pint of cold water into a saucepan, add to this a piece of carpenter's glue about the size of a hazel-nut, and place on the fire to heat. Put three teaspoonfuls of flour into a basin and, with *cold* water, mix to a smooth paste. When the water in the saucepan boils, add it to the paste, stirring well all the time. Then place the mixture in the saucepan and boil for about two minutes. Leave till cold. Always brush with the way of the material and put on thinly and evenly with a finger.

Shoemaker's paste made from rye flour can be used, but it must be fresh and is very strong. The paste must be allowed to become stiff before being used.

The materials from which the patterns are to be cut should be pinned face downwards on to a flat surface. (A large cork mat or a wooden table is excellent for this.) The paste is brushed over lightly and evenly on the wrong side; it must on no account be allowed to soak through to the front of the material; it should be allowed to become perfectly dry before moving. The patterns may then be cut out and tacked to their foundation and in time it will be found that the stiffening paste has disappeared in the course of wear and washing. It is only necessary to prepare materials in this way when the patterns are to be applied with stitching over a raw edge; for those in which the edges are turned in, it is not only unnecessary but would make the sewing much more difficult to do.

The preparation of cut-out patterns in which the edges to be turned in is simple. Cutting is done with allowance for turnings and these are tacked down as a narrow hem at the edges, on the wrong side of the material. In the case of fabric with a glazed surface, the tacking should be kept to the back of the work. (See Appendix B, p. 167.)

PLANNING A COVERLET

The planning of a coverlet in applied work needs forethought. Each part of the pattern must be placed with an eye to the general balance and when their positions are decided it is well to indicate them by marking, before they are tacked and finally sewn. Many of the old coverlets were first "quartered" before the designing was begun. The foundation material was folded in half and then in half again and the creases marked with a line of stitching. A fourth part of the design was then arranged within the area of one quarter; this was repeated four times, with a resulting whole that was well balanced. Other arrangements, by the more artistically gifted workers, with a natural sense of proportion and spacing, were done "by eye".

In any case, whichever the means used to decide on the placing of the design, the next stage of the work—the preparatory setting of the applied patterns on to the foundation—if successfully done, is more than half the battle won. Setting, the process in which the patterns are temporarily fixed in place, was usually carried out by means of tacking which was withdrawn when the final sewing was completed.

In referring to methods of attaching applied patterns in embroidery, Margaret Jourdain says[1]: "The applications were, as a rule, sewn, though it was sometimes thought sufficient to stick them to their foundations with glue or some similar substance." This could only have been possible if heavy or unwashable materials, such as velvet, were part of the pattern and there is no precedent for it in applied patchwork. Indeed, as far as this is concerned it is a practice better forgotten than copied; any sticking of the patterns to the foundation can be only temporary and must be an

[1] *English Secular Embroidery*, p. 19.

alternative to tacking and a preliminary to sewing. The use of a slight application of the stiffening paste has been justified as a means of anchoring some patterns lightly to the background, when the material would otherwise be defaced by tacking marks. Traces of it can be seen on the back of some coverlets which are still unused or unwashed, but no temporary sticking is as satisfactory a method as tacking. The paste makes the work stiff to handle (unless very skilfully applied) and interferes with the smooth working of the needle.

Once the patterns are in place the final sewing is done by the traditional methods of *hemming*, *herringboning* or *buttonholing*.

In applied work, hemming can be used on all patterns which will retain a good outline after a turning has been made. The shape of the pattern also depends on the worker's skill in turning the hem. In some cases the shape is happily ignored and hemming is used on any outline because it is a familiar process and therefore easy to do, whether the pattern calls for it or not. This is roughly effective, but can in no way compare with the careful work in the majority of quilts and coverlets.

The most straightforward patterns are those which consist of units or groups of geometrical patches, applied directly to the foundation after they have been joined together and the papers removed.

Leaf and flower patterns, shaped with the aid of a template and cut out of cotton dress fabrics, are usually attached with hemming. These are softer to handle than many furnishing materials and with them it is comparatively simple to manipulate a turning in the angle of a leaf or the curve of a stem.

Any patterns with a curved outline can be made with greater accuracy if Method I in the making of *Shell* patches is adoped, substituting the shell template for one appropriate to the shape required (Appendix C). The patterns in the "Isle of Wight" quilt and many other similar ones were probably shaped in this way, before being hemmed to the foundation (*131*).

Another method, which has come to be known as *blind* or *invisible* hemming, is found in patterns suitable for ordinary hemming. It is somewhat similar to a *slip-stitch* and is worked under the fold, instead of on the edge. The stitches are closely spaced instead of being at long intervals as in *slip-stitch* and the turned hem and the flat of the material are caught together in one movement, as for ordinary hemming. The advantage is that, although the sewing is done on the face of the work, the stitches can only be seen on the wrong side, which adds considerably to the good appearance of the work.

Herringbone is another stitch employed in plain sewing. It resembles *cross-stitch* in appearance and is used extensively in *crazy* patchwork for covering the joining stitches. Here it is only decorative in intention, but in applied work it is the means by which the patterns are attached to the foundation. The edges of the cut-out patterns are left raw and the pieces are laid flat for tacking into position. *Herringbone-stitch* is then worked over the edges and the tacking stitches are ultimately removed. This stitch can be used to apply almost any kind of pattern and is invariably worked in white or natural cotton or linen sewing thread. The latticed effect made by the herringboning softens the outline, especially in the heavier kinds of pattern. This is particularly so in the "Prince of Wales' Feathers" quilt (*162*).

Buttonhole-stitch is one that is in common use and needs little description. It is sometimes called *loop-stitch* (to distinguish it from that used on a *tailor's buttonhole*, which has a twisted edge) and is so called because it is the buttonhole stitch with which the strands of a button-loop are covered. It is worked from left to right.

In applied work it has been used as a traditional means of attaching patterns in which the raw edges are left unfolded. The stitches should be spaced evenly and yet be close enough together to hide the material underneath. They should on no account be crowded together, as this tends to cut the materials and cause them to pull away from the foundation.

The traditional thread is coloured sewing silk but the work has frequently been done in white or natural-coloured cotton or linen thread. The silk usually carries out the general colour of the fabric patterns and in some coverlets each colour change in the patterns is matched with a similar change of colour in the silk. Thus, a bouquet containing red, blue and pink flowers with shades of green in the leaves would be matched with red, blue, pink and green sewing silks, wherever these colours appeared on the edge of the pattern. In other instances the patterns are buttonholed with one colour, sometimes of a dark shade, so that the patterns are heavily outlined and appear to stand away from the background.

The preliminary setting of the patterns is done with tacking; this is carried out, just inside the outline of the shape, in the same coloured sewing silk as that with which the buttonholing is to be done. In this work the tackings are left in and are covered by the buttonhole stitches; if they are run in a sufficiently even distance from the edge, they can be used to gauge the depth of the buttonholing.

The outline produced by the loops of the stitches should be unbroken, except where the pattern demands it. The joining-on of a fresh thread tends to make a break in this outline, unless care is taken to prevent it. The end of the old thread should be drawn back through the last stitches which were made; it should not be pulled tightly but left with a loop, which can be held down by the thumb of the left hand. The new thread is then run back from the unstitched edge and the needle brought up through the loop of the old thread. This loop is then gently drawn through until the new thread lies snugly within it—it should not be drawn too tightly—and the end is then trimmed off. The buttonholing is continued.

It is unwise to attempt a join on a corner or in a difficult turn of the pattern.

INLAY

Inlay is rarely used in patchwork; it is almost impossible to do with materials which tend to fray and for this reason it is usually made of felt. It is possible to prevent a certain amount of fraying by pasting the wrong side of the materials, as in onlaid appliqué, but this makes the pieces stiff to handle and it is better to choose materials which do not fray in the first place. The fitting pieces of the pattern can be tacked on to a *temporary* background of calico, linen or holland, but each must be cut with great precision, so that there are no spaces between them. The joining is often done by overcasting on the right side and the joins subsequently covered by a cord, but in the coverlet at Overbecks and the one made by James Williams (*156*) the edges are seamed on the wrong side. It is important that the surface is perfectly smooth except for the overlaid cord where it is used. To thicken a thin material for use with a thick one, it may be lined with scrim or other suitable material before cutting out the pattern.

INDEX

INDEX

The numerals in **heavy** type denote the figure numbers of the illustrations